Written Communication for GAMSAT:
A step by step approach

Eira Makepeace

Written Communication for GAMSAT: A step by step approach

Spine Publishing, Dr Prep Ltd, CPC1, Capital Park, Cambridge, CB21 5XE

© Eira Makepeace 2011

British Library Cataloguing in Publication Data

A catalogue record for this book is available from the British Library

ISBN 978-0-9551325-7-5

Cover design by Dawn Sellars

Contents

Contributors

With sincere thanks to:

Gemma Ames

Nadine Bhugagee

Douglas Corrigall

Poojya Manjunath

Lamia Nayeb

Jennifer Peycke

Sarah Sharp

Olivia Stredder

Foreword

Nail-bitingly nervous and waiting to go into the test centre, I overheard a woman comment to her friend: "Section 2 of the GAMSAT is the hardest section, but it's the one you can't prepare for. In fact, practising just wastes time, as you don't know what the topic will be before you go in." This is the biggest fallacy about Section 2 of the GAMSAT. Without practice, I could never have passed the essay questions, let alone done well enough to compete against the hundreds of intelligent people taking the test. In fact, the most important piece of advice anyone ever gave me was practice, practice, practice. To pass this test, you have to want to pass it desperately. This is easy to say, but when it means writing an essay a day, no matter how exhausted you are from a day at work or hung over from the night before, even the most ardent would-be doctor must be daunted.

The other fallacy is the idea that arts students have an advantage over science students. In theory, this could be true because arts students are used to essay writing and the discipline of expressing abstract ideas in a coherent and engaging way. I am a graduate in English Literature, and I was secretly hoping this would give me an advantage, a reason to do less preparation. However, after my first attempt at a practice essay I realised my mistake. Arts essays are generally longer and therefore can be less concise. They rarely, if ever, make use of the personal element which is crucial in GAMSAT essays, more often relying on research which can take months to complete. In addition, the criteria by which they are marked may be entirely different to those used by the examining body for GAMSAT. So science students don't be daunted and arts students don't be complacent. My philosophy after my first essay writing experience for GAMSAT was to forget my usual methods in favour of a new approach more focused on the appropriate marking criteria and honed by many practice essays.

I started to prepare for the essay writing section of the test about six weeks before the exam. From the beginning I decided to stick to the time limits for essay writing. 30 minutes is a very short time in which to write an essay, and this fact intimidated me from the start. On the plus side, that writing a timed essay could take no more than 30 minutes encouraged me to do the practice even when I was exhausted and would rather be somewhere else! I wrote out my aims on a piece of paper in front of me, as specified in Eira's preparation course:

- Clear opening
- Theme well developed
- Balance of ideas
- Assertions exemplified
- Conclusion drawn from the text or data
- Insight displayed
- Varied vocabulary
- Varied expression
- Varied sentences

I looked at them from time to time whilst writing to make sure I was meeting all the criteria. After I had written four or five practice essays, I no longer needed to look at the aims but I continually made a mental check that I was meeting them all. I then set myself the task of writing two essays a week for the six weeks before the exam and one a day for the entire week before the exam. On the day before the exam I gave myself a timed practice by writing two essays in one hour. This is actually a big challenge - maintaining the energy to write two excellent essays back to back is exhausting and it is difficult to switch subjects as quickly as this requires.

It was surprisingly easy to find quotations from which to write my essays. Type "travel quotes", "courage quotes", "happiness quotes" or any other theme into Google and hundreds of thousands of helpful pages appear. Emotions or personal qualities work well as themes, but any general topic you can think of will be sufficient as a practice essay. In terms of marking my work, I occasionally let my friends or family critique the essays but mostly I judged them myself against the marking criteria. I also found that the process of writing these essays helped me to develop a structure that I could stick to. This meant that when I got to the actual exam, I felt I was able to concentrate on the content of the essay instead of worrying about the structure.

Sitting in the exam hall, I was very glad I had done the preparation. It had felt like a lot of work at the time and I wasn't always sure exactly how to rate my progress, but the simple fact that I had learnt how to structure an essay and complete it in the allotted time ensured there were no surprises on the day and I felt relatively confident in my ability.

Don't be daunted! Essay writing is a skill which can be learnt with lots of practice and determination. Good luck!

Olivia Stredder, BA hons Lond
Medical Student

Introduction

Writing essays for admissions tests: general principles

The principles below are general to most forms of writing and can be adapted to suit other admissions tests that include an essay. Later chapters will focus on the essays to be written for GAMSAT.

1. The rules of the game

Think of a game like football or chess. What do they have in common? The purpose is to win and they both have rules by which the game must be played. Writing an essay is rather like a game in some respects. The essay game is not for amusement or diversion but is a serious undertaking that has to follow certain rules if you are to write a good enough essay to achieve your purpose, which is entry into medical school. This chapter will introduce you to most of the rules of the essay game.

2. The elements of essay writing

All good writing contains certain elements and most errors in writing come from ignoring one or more of these elements. This section looks at the elements that need to be considered when producing any piece of writing but particularly in your essays for GAMSAT.

2.1 Audience

Writing is meant to be read. The audience can be teachers, examiners, friends and family, editors and publishers or employers. You have to consider your audience when writing; you would not write a chatty letter to a potential employer and you would not write a formal letter to a friend. In most cases, we have a sense of our audience when we write and usually instinctively choose the right way to write for them. Occasionally we lapse and do not chose the right 'register' or the language that is most suitable for our purpose. Later we will explore more closely the audience you will be writing for in your GAMSAT essays.

2.2 Purpose

The purpose of writing can be to entertain, to inform, to persuade someone to a particular view, to expound on a subject or to instruct. Most writing can be put into one or more of these categories.

2.3 Length of piece

Writing can be limited by word length, page length or by time. In twenty minutes you can write by hand approximately a side and a half of A4 provided you have done the necessary planning.

2.4 Structure

The structure of an essay is the way in which your thoughts are organised. This organisation is done through careful paragraphing. There will be more about paragraphing later.

2.5 Balance of ideas

It is a good idea when writing a formal essay to have some balance to your ideas. This means that when taking a particular perspective you also give an alternative viewpoint - if you give a view about an issue, you also need to give a counter-argument.

2.6 Explanation, evidence and examples

It is not enough to state a point; you must also explain it, provide evidence for your perspective and illustrate that you understand the point you are making through appropriate examples. Thus, if you say you are opposed to experiments performed on animals, you need to explain why you hold this view and give an example to show that similar results can be obtained by other means. In an essay for academic purposes, you would need to provide research or other evidence for your views.

2.7 Expression

Expression is the use you make of language. People usually develop their own writing style so it is important to ensure that your style is fluent and reads smoothly, that you use a wide vocabulary and that your writing is grammatically correct. If English is not your first language, an International

Testing System score of at least 6.5, or an equivalent, would suggest the necessary level of competence in English.

Your expression does not need to be complex. If you are not confident use shorter, simpler sentences; long sentences with multiple clauses hold traps for the unwary. Only use words if you know their meaning. If, however, you can write fluently with no errors, or if you use language confidently and easily, stick to your own style of writing.

Sentences need to be varied in length. Short sentences throughout an essay will soon tire the reader as will long sentences. Try starting with different words or in different ways so that there is some variety in your sentence construction. Similarly, try to use different words for the same meaning rather than repeat the same word in your writing. For example instead of the word 'suggest' as in 'This title suggests...' you can use 'states' 'asserts', 'evokes', 'implies' or 'alludes to'.
Slang and colloquial expressions are best avoided in formal writing. It is not 'cool' to write a 'fun' essay for examination purposes; stick to conventional English unless you are using direct speech.

2.8 Spelling and grammar
Examiners are much more forgiving about spelling errors than they were in the past as long as the errors do not interfere with the writer's meaning. However, a correctly spelled essay is more pleasant to read, as the reader is not jarred or jolted by the error. The reader wants to enter into the essay alongside the writer rather than be drawn up short by a spelling mistake or other breach of convention.

Grammatically correct sentences are easier to read than those whose meaning is obscured by faulty grammar. There are many ways to polish up your grammar but perhaps the best way to improve grammar, spelling and vocabulary is to read widely and to read through a style guide. Some references are given at the end of this chapter.

2.9 Presentation

Presentation matters. It is much easier to read and mark a well set out essay with clearly spaced paragraphs, legible handwriting and little, if any, crossing out. Far too many candidates forget about this aspect of their essay and hand in illegible work, with dense, un-paragraphed writing and numerous crossings out. If the work is planned properly, there will be much less need to strike out words, clauses or paragraphs and each of the paragraphs will indicate a new or further thought. Indentation of paragraphs is not necessary but a space between paragraphs is ideal.

3. GAMSAT essay writing elements

In this section, we will look briefly at the elements of essay writing specific to GAMSAT.

3.1 Audience

For GAMSAT your audience is the examiner who marks your script. There are some important things to know about examiners: they will use an agreed mark scheme, this mark scheme will be based on the assessment criteria published, their marks will be agreed with a moderator, each script may be marked by more than one examiner and the scripts are anonymous. Examiners are trained to assess the merits of each essay; they will be able to spot flaws in arguments, weaknesses in the use of language and sloppy or vague expression. Since examiners are first and foremost readers, they will have the same prejudices as any other readers, irritation at poorly presented work and illegible handwriting and despair of unparagraphed work. The examiners will have hundreds of essays to mark in a very short period of time so you will be repaid if you take care over presentation.

3.2 Purpose

The word essay comes from the French *essayer* 'to try' or attempt to come to a view about a topic. From your attempt, the examiners and admissions tutors will be able to determine your general intellectual ability, your communication skills, and your ability to develop a coherent set of ideas according to a brief. It is important, therefore, that you demonstrate these abilities and skills as well as you can in the essay.

3.3 The brief

It is crucial that you work to the brief, the essay topic set. Many candidates fail to answer the brief and so do not do well. Careful planning can help you to stay focussed on your topic and hence avoid this all too common problem.

The brief is specific to each examination. There are distinct types of essay, personal and reflective, expository and discursive, and analysis and synthesis of data, so you need to know the type of response required for each essay type.

Expository or discursive requires an objective account of your perspective on a particular topic, for example your views on the place of sport in schools or the use of animal models in the development of new drugs. Some points for and against the proposal are expected and necessary and a conclusion based on your material is essential.

A reflective essay requires a personal point of view and is usually based upon your own experience or that of someone you know well. The experience must be described and some reflection on what the experience meant to you and others needs to be recorded. In particular, the lesson learned from the experience and how it has been applied to your life, especially with regard to your interaction with other people, must be included.

For GAMSAT, there is no requirement to analyse or synthesise from data provided.

3.4 Assessment criteria

Since your examiners will be marking your script according to certain criteria, it is essential that you know what is expected. The criteria are set out on the GAMSAT website (www.gamsatuk.org) and shown below and should be clearly understood and perhaps memorised. The criteria can be considered vague enough to be worrying but this vagueness offers plenty of scope for all candidates to write an interesting essay.

CRITERIA FOR THE ASSESSMENT OF WRITTEN COMMUNICATION
Assessors consider the following issues:
Thought and Content
(the quality of what is said)
- what is made of and developed from the task
- the kinds of thought and feeling offered in response to the task

Organisation and Expression
(the quality of the structure developed and the language used)
- the shape and form of the piece
- the effectiveness and fluency of the language

3.5 Place of the essay in the exam
Know the weight given to each section of the exam, as this will indicate the amount of effort you need to put into your revision. The weighting of the various components is set out on the GAMSAT website (www.gamsatuk.org) and in their printed material. If writing essays is one of your strengths but you are concerned about other aspects, you do not need to revise as much for your essay writing. If, on the other hand, you have not written essays for some time or think you are weak in this discipline, you need to spend more time practising.

3.6 The time limit
The time limit for each essay is 30 minutes. With practice, it is perfectly possible to plan and write up to one and half sides of A4 in five or six paragraphs including the introduction and conclusion in this time.

3.7 Organisation
Organisation or structure refers to the way your thoughts are organised and set down on the page. A well-structured essay has a clear introduction leading to several interlocking paragraphs and is rounded off with a conclusion drawn from the preceding paragraphs. It should be evident to your reader that your thoughts are developing in a logical way so the conclusion comes as no surprise. This does not mean, however, that your

essay will be dull or pedestrian as a result; there is always opportunity for a sting in the tail in an unexpected conclusion.

3.8 Balance of ideas

You must try to give a balanced perspective especially in the expository essay for GAMSAT. Even in the reflective essay, a balanced view should be offered. An essay full of polemic (where only one point of view is expressed) is not balanced and therefore does not have a pleasing shape.

3.9 Examples and evidence

Including examples as evidence is the simplest way to show the examiner you know what you are writing about and adds freshness and originality. Given how many essays your examiner has to mark, all essentially on the same topic, a well chosen example can be very helpful. Make sure that your example does illustrate and explain your point; perhaps use something like, "This shows..." or "This illustrates..." to highlight this.

3.10 Other considerations

All the elements above, expression, vocabulary, sentence construction, spelling and grammar hold true for any admission test essay, as do presentation, the appearance of the essay, paragraph spacing and general tidiness.

In the next chapter we will explore the mechanics of writing essays in more detail.

References

William Strunk Jnr, editor E.B White (1999) The Elements of Style, Longman

The Economist Style Guide (2005) Profile Books Ltd.

The Timed Essay

The 30 minute timed essay: details and worked example

This section will show you, step by step, a conventional way of writing a timed essay for an admissions test using a worked example. You will not be expected to possess specialist knowledge on the themes of the essays but you will need to be able to draw on your experience and general knowledge. Further worked examples specific to GAMSAT will follow in later chapters.

1. Starting off

1.1 The instructions

Imagine you are turning over your essay question paper in a test. You will see some instructions giving you the time limit and the number of questions to answer. These may be called writing tasks. Even if you have practised writing numerous essays, take time to read all the instructions and make sure you follow them.

1.2 The brief and its meaning (3 minutes planning)

It is absolutely critical that your essay responds to the brief and nothing but the brief. To ensure that you are clear about the meaning of the brief, underline the key words.

For example:

1. <u>Old</u> dogs <u>cannot learn</u> <u>new</u> tricks
The keywords here are "old", "cannot learn" and "new" so they need to be underlined.
2. <u>All experimentation</u> upon <u>animals</u> is <u>wrong</u>
3. <u>Distance</u> is a great <u>promoter</u> of <u>admiration</u>

The next thing to do is to decipher the meaning of the brief. To do this, you need to rephrase the quotation or sentence or explain it to yourself.

"<u>Old </u>dogs <u>cannot learn</u> <u>new</u> tricks" means literally that old dogs cannot be taught how to perform new tricks but this is not the only meaning of the sentence. It is usually shorthand for the purported difficulty older people have in learning new skills and suggests that there is something inherent in older people that prevents them from doing so. Hence this essay is going to be a discussion about whether or not it is possible for older people to learn new things and what hinders or helps them to learn new ways of thinking, doing or being.

"<u>All experimentation</u> upon <u>animals</u> is <u>wrong</u>" means exactly what it says: that it is wrong in all cases to experiment upon animals irrespective of the kind of experiment or potential benefit to animals or human beings. It is an unequivocal statement lending itself to an essay that will argue for and against animal experimentation; it is a "Yes but, no but" essay.

"<u>Distance</u> is a great <u>promoter</u> of <u>admiration</u>" is a variation of another quotation "distance lends enchantment to the view" and means that the further we are away from something, the more attractive it is. It can be applied in many circumstances, our view of an historical event or period, a person we would not get on with at close quarters or a person from another time or place whose flaws are not as apparent as they would be on closer inspection. This essay is going to discuss the extent to which this quotation can be true in all circumstances.

Having underlined the key words and deciphered the meaning of the topic, the next step is to brainstorm some ideas. Bearing in mind you have just a few minutes for the planning, you do not need very many ideas or points.

1.3 Brainstorming ideas (4-7 minutes)
You can approach brainstorming in different ways. Essentially, you come up with some uncensored ideas, examine them and keep the ones that will be most useful. The ideas can be scribbled down in a column, a table or a mind map.

Let us take the first example, "Old dogs cannot learn new tricks" and brainstorm some ideas using the meaning older people cannot learn new skills.

Old people can't learn new things *For the proposition*	Old people can learn new things *Against the proposition*
1. Technology e.g. the DVD recorder 2. Stick in the mud e.g. no further learning, old fashioned clothing, cooking etc 3. Clashes with children	1. But plenty of 'silver surfers' 2. Professional updating e.g. doctors, lawyers, adult education flourishes 3. Learn from children

You now have six points you can use in your essay but you may not have time to use them all so choose four you can write about comfortably in the time available. I would choose technology as there are points for and against old people's ability to use new technology and then pick any three other points. Perhaps the most to be gained from this essay topic is a discussion of learning and particularly the place of lifelong learning whether formal or informal.

Each point can be expressed in one paragraph so, with your introduction and conclusion, you have five or six paragraphs to write.

1.4 Paragraphing
The conventions of paragraphing are straightforward; one thought per paragraph is the rule. The thought can be explained, expanded and exemplified in three separate sentences.

Examples of:
Explaining words: means, represents, suggests, portrays, alludes to, depicts, connotes, refers to.

Expanding words: implies, displays, demonstrates, signifies, indicates. You can also use words from the *Explaining* list above.

Exemplifying words: for example, for instance, in this case, take the case of, in another case, on this occasion, in this situation, to demonstrate, an illustration, to illustrate, as an illustration.

Paragraph linking words:
Good writing links thoughts together in individual paragraphs and these paragraphs must then be linked together to carry your thoughts forward to

the conclusion. Linking words are important as they act as *signals* or *signposts* to your reader and show the direction you are intending to take. There are numerous words you can use to link your propositions for and against the meaning or implication of a theme.

For the proposition: in addition to, moreover, also, as well as, again, and then, besides, equally important, finally, further, furthermore, too, next, last, what is more, first (second, etc.),

Against the proposition: on the other hand, but, however, whereas, yet, nevertheless, on the contrary, by comparison, where, compared to, up against, balanced against, vis à vis, although, conversely, meanwhile, after all, in contrast, although this may be true.

Exception to the propositions for and against: yet, still, however, nevertheless, in spite of, despite, of course, once in a while, sometimes.

Concluding words: in brief, on the whole, summing up, to conclude, in conclusion, as I have shown, as I have said, hence, therefore, accordingly, thus, as a result, consequently.

1.5 The introduction (3 minutes)
In an essay for academic purposes, you would usually draft the essay before writing your introduction but there is no time for this approach in a timed essay so you will have to start your essay with the introduction and then write the body.

Introducing words: means, suggests, depicts, portrays, alludes to, explores.

1.6 Worked example

We're going to use the quotation "*You cannot teach old dogs new tricks*"

a) Introduction (first paragraph)

The easiest way to start this essay is to *explain, expand* and *exemplify* the meaning of the topic. We can expand the meaning by giving an additional statement such as the circumstances in which the statement is usually applied (this will also give us an *example),* whether it is usually used positively or negatively and what it reveals about the people who use it.

"This statement means literally that old dogs cannot be taught how to perform new tricks but this is not the only meaning of the statement. It is usually shorthand for the difficulty older people are thought to have in learning new skills and suggests that there is something inherent in older people that prevents them from learning (**expansion**). It is often used in recruitment when employers are prejudiced about employing older people or can be used to imply that retraining people is a waste of time and money (**example**). The assertion is almost always used negatively and although it may be true in some circumstances, it is certainly true that older people can learn new skills" (*this sentence suggests the writer's view and gives an indication of the conclusion).*

[There is also an issue of language here: what is meant by old? Is it a fixed age or stage of life or an attitude? We might want to say what we mean by old and that this interpretation is the basis for the term, "old" in our essay.]

From this introduction, our reader can tell that we are going to discuss how the statement can be true and in what circumstances it is false. The reader can tell from our examples that we have a view but that we are going to be fair and balanced and deal with both sides of the argument. The reader is also clear that you understand the meaning of the proverb or statement.

b) Second paragraph (5 minutes)

In this paragraph we are going to raise our first point. It will be better to give all the points supporting the meaning of the statement (older people cannot lean new skills) in the first two paragraphs so that subsequent paragraphs argue against the truth of the statement (older people can indeed learn new skills). That way, the conclusion implied in the introduction will follow on logically, namely that it is not always true that older people cannot learn new skills.

Again, we will state the point, expand it and give an example to show we know what we are talking about. In this case, we are going to start with the idea that there is truth in the statement. For example:

"It is undoubtedly true that it is harder to learn some new skills as one grows older. This may be because the skills require some physical attribute that one has never possessed or that there is no previous learning to associate with the new skills. For instance, it is a longstanding joke that children find it easier to programme video recorders than their parents and it may well be true that older people find the array of new technology bewildering or find it difficult to adapt to some aspects of contemporary life such as mastering chip and pin credit cards or internet banking. It is possibly also true that some older people simply do not bother to learn new skills or ways of thinking as it is too much effort or requires shifts in views with which they are not comfortable."

c) Third paragraph (5 minutes)

This paragraph follows the formula of the previous paragraph with a second example to support the meaning of the quotation. We will make our point, expand it and give an example.

"Another area where it is evident that older people have not learned new tricks or adapted to changes in society is seen in the attitudes they have towards some aspects of their children's live. Parents may have been brought up to respect their elders whereas this may not be true for their children, who may have been taught to think for themselves and believe that respect must be earned rather than given solely on the grounds of age. Older people may find the clothes that younger people wear ugly or unflattering while they may be wearing clothes that younger people consider unfashionable. These examples show the differences in values held by older people and they are the hardest to change as they mean that something dear to the individual has to change, that something is given up or so older people fear. Attitudes and values are the hardest things to change and it may be that this is a new trick too far for many."

d) Fourth paragraph (5 minutes)

This paragraph begins the counter-argument where propositions to rebut the topic's assertions are raised. Good words with which to start this paragraph include, "however", nevertheless", and "on the other hand". Referring to our brainstorm ideas, we will use two of the most telling points, such as older people who have got to grips with new technology in a variety of settings and who continue learning in formal and informal settings. Again, explain and exemplify. For example:

"On the other hand, we can see that many older people have embraced new technology to the extent that they are called 'silver surfers' and there are even dating agencies for people in this group. Daytime courses related to information technology abound in numerous settings across the UK; regular updating and training for employees needing to use the latest software is available and a multitude of learning opportunities exist specifically for older people **(examples)**. Further, for older people whose professional world changes frequently due to advances in knowledge or legislation, there is no choice but to adapt by learning **(explanation)**. Doctors, for example, have to adjust to changes in clinical practise while lawyers must adapt to changes in law **(examples)**. Then there are also those older people who have to retrain to take advantage of new developments or who never trained in the first place **(explanation)**. The Open University was established precisely to provide educational opportunities for older people and it has flourished since its establishment." **(example)**

e) Conclusion (2-3 minutes)

Now we are ready to write the conclusion to our essay. This can be a summary of the material, a standard approach, or we can aim for something that consolidates what we have written and adds a twist. The main point is that, whatever the approach, the conclusion must be based on the work so far rather than appear to be tacked on as an afterthought. Remember, only one conclusion is permitted. For example:

"From the above, it is evident that the assertion of the topic does not hold true for all older people assuming one could define this group accurately. Many older people do indeed adapt to changes in society and some even embrace them. Those who do not adjust or adapt do not suffer from some inherent inability to learn, rather they may not have had the right opportunity or access to new technology or simply see no need for change. The sales of brain games seem to suggest that some people do see the need to learn new skills and these people are likely to be older rather than younger."

f) The completed essay

"This statement means literally that old dogs cannot be taught how to perform new tricks but this is not the only meaning of the statement. It is usually shorthand for the difficulty older people are thought to have in learning new skills and suggests that there is something inherent in older people that prevents them from learning. It is often used in recruitment when employers are prejudiced about employing older people or can be used to imply that retraining people is a waste of time and money. The assertion is almost always used negatively and although it may be true in some circumstances, it is certainly true that older people can learn new skills.

It is undoubtedly true that it is harder to learn some new skills as one grows older. This may be because the skills require some physical attribute that one has never possessed or that there is no previous learning to associate with the new skills. For instance, it is a longstanding joke that children find it easier to programme video recorders than their parents and it may well be true that older people find the array of new technology bewildering or find it difficult to adapt to some aspects of contemporary life such as mastering chip and pin credit cards or internet banking. It is possibly also true that some older people simply do not bother to learn new skills or ways of thinking as it is too much effort or requires shifts in views with which they are not comfortable.

Another area where it is evident that older people have not learned new tricks or adapted to changes in society is seen in the attitudes they have towards aspects of their children's live. Parents may have been brought up to respect their elders whereas this may not be true for their children, who may have been taught to think for themselves and believe that respect must be earned rather than given solely on the grounds of age. Older people may find the clothes that younger people wear ugly or unflattering while they may be wearing clothes that younger people consider unfashionable. These examples show the differences in values held by older people and they are the hardest to change as they mean that something dear to the individual has to change, that something is given up or so older people fear. Attitudes and values are the hardest things to change and it may be that this is a new trick too far for many.

On the other hand, we can see that many older people have embraced new technology to the extent that they are called 'silver surfers' and there are even dating agencies for people in this group. Daytime courses related to information technology abound in numerous settings across the UK; regular updating and training for employees needing to use the latest software is available and a multitude of learning opportunities exist specifically for older people. Further, for older people whose professional world changes frequently due to advances in knowledge or legislation, there is no choice but to adapt by learning. Doctors, for example, have to adjust to changes in clinical practise while lawyers must adapt to changes in law. Then there are also those older people who have to retrain to take advantage of new developments or who never trained in the first place. The Open University was established precisely to provide educational opportunities for older people and it has flourished since its establishment.

From the above, it is evident that the assertion of the topic does not hold true for all older people assuming one could define this group accurately. Many older people do indeed adapt to changes in society and some even embrace them. Those who do not adjust or adapt do not suffer from some inherent inability to learn, rather they may not have had the right opportunity, or access to new technology or simply see no need for change. The sales of brain games seem to *suggest that some people do see the need to learn new skills and these people are likely to be older rather than younger."* (690 words)

How to improve your writing

1. Wide reading is one important way in which you can improve your writing. If you have no time to read books, try reading articles or commentaries in quality newspapers or journals; these often resemble essays in their structure.

2. Practise reading your work aloud so that your ear helps you detect any clumsiness or woolly thought. Asking friends or family to read your work will also help.

3. Writing an essay a week by hand before your test is useful. It is not a large amount of time to give up and the benefits will be obvious as you sharpen your writing skills.

4. There are many websites that offer essay-writing skills . These may be worth visiting although mostly they are intended for people who have to research a topic then write it up. Nevertheless, some useful tips may be gained from these websites.

5. Courses such as those provided by Dr Prep Ltd (www.drprep.net) can be useful to hone your skills and provide feedback.

Timed essays for GAMSAT: additional rules

This chapter examines in detail the *additional* rules of essay writing for GAMSAT. These concern:

1. the purpose of the essay
2. the requirements of the two types of essay or writing tasks
3. the assessment criteria.

For GAMSAT, two essay tests form the "written communication" element. An example of each type of essay will be worked through here and examples of good and poor GAMSAT essays will be included in the later chapters with a commentary on their respective strengths and weaknesses.

The writing tests

On your examination sheet the two writing tasks are likely to be called "Writing Test A" and "Writing Test B". You will be given a number of prompts in the form of quotations around a common theme and will be required to write your essay in response to *one or more of them.* You are not required to give a title to your essay or to say to which quotations you are responding. However, to do so is sensible as it helps to orient you as well as your reader towards the topic of your essay.

1. The purpose of the essay

According to the information on the GAMSAT website, the purpose of the written communication section is to assess whether you can "organise and express your thoughts in a logical and effective way". I have already touched on organisation (the structure of the essay), expression (your use of language) and the logical development of your thoughts (through points made in each paragraph) but these will be covered in greater depth in this chapter.

2. The structure and content of the test

The website describes the detail of the test in the link on structure and content.

The Written Communication section is a test of the ability to produce and develop ideas in writing. It involves two thirty-minute writing tasks. Each task offers a number of ideas relating to a common theme. The theme will be general rather than specific in nature. The first task deals with <u>socio-cultural</u> issues while the second deals with more <u>personal issues</u>. In selecting topics for the writing tasks every effort is made to minimise factors which might disadvantage candidates from non-English-speaking backgrounds.

From this detail we learn three useful points.
a) Firstly, whilst the themes could be on almost any of a wide range of topics, the environment, science and technology, education, health and so on, the key point is that the topics set will have some theme in common.

b) The second important point to note is that there are two types of essays (called writing tasks by GAMSAT) to be written in two thirty-minute periods. You will need to be clear about the distinction between the types of essay and to make sure you can write well in both genres.

3. GAMSAT writing task assessment criteria

The criteria against which you will be assessed are as important as all the other constraints put together. You can write a brilliantly crafted essay but will fail if you do not meet the assessment criteria. As with the other GAMSAT constraints, you must pay careful attention to the criteria for assessment and ensure you know what they mean.

The ACER website states the criteria twice. The first statement gives them in outline and the second, in table form, expands the criteria. You need to be thoroughly familiar with the expanded criteria.

From the Acer website, 'info book' link below

(http://www.gamsatuk.org/documents/GAMSATUKIBSEP07.pdf)

Criteria in outline

"Written Communication is assessed on two criteria. These criteria address the quality of the thinking about a topic and the control of language demonstrated in its development. Assessment focuses on the way in which ideas are integrated into a thoughtful response to the task. Control of language (grammatical structure and expression) is an integral component of a good piece of writing. However, it is only assessed insofar as it contributes to the overall effectiveness of the response to the task and not in isolation. Candidates are not assessed on the 'correctness' of the ideas or attitudes they display."

3.1 Quality of the thinking

This criterion is expressed twice: once it is described as "quality of thinking" and then it is described as the way your "ideas are integrated into a thoughtful response to the task". In essence this means a logically developed, coherent, consistently argued piece of work. Quality of thought is demonstrated by moving through an essay in such a way that your reader can follow easily in your footsteps and see how you reached your conclusion. It can mean challenging accepted wisdom about a topic, explaining and justifying your assertions, but always giving a balanced view. A thoughtful response raises each point clearly and these points fit with the theme and the perspective you are taking. It means that you show that you have given the topic some thought and that you are able to argue from different standpoints. It also means that your conclusion follows from all the preceding work.

3.2 Control of language

Control of language is closely allied to quality of thought; woolly writing stems from woolly thinking. Think a sentence through before you write so that you choose precisely the right words to express your intended meaning. However, from the outline criteria above, we can see that control of language is important *only* if it contributes to the general effectiveness of the piece. This suggests that imperfect language will not be penalised as heavily as a response lacking thought would be. Nevertheless, control of language is clearly important as it is through your language that you can express your "thoughtfulness".

3.3 The criteria in detail

CRITERIA FOR THE ASSESSMENT OF WRITTEN COMMUNICATION

Raters consider the following issues:

Thought and Content
(the quality of what is said)
• **what is made of and developed from the task**
• **the kinds of thought and feeling offered in response to the task**

Organisation and Expression
(the quality of the structure developed and the language used)
• **the shape and form of the piece**
• **the effectiveness and fluency of the language**

3.3.1 Thought and content
a) What is made of and developed from the task
This is rather vague for our purposes but it means the extent to which you have taken the theme and developed a coherent, balanced set of ideas relating to the theme of one or more of the quotations.

b) The kinds of thought and feeling offered in response to the task
Again, this does not offer you the specific guidance you might wish for. Equally, the lack of specificity is on your side as it means you will be judged on the depth of your thinking about the theme. Your perspective on the subject, the arguments and counter-arguments you offer will be important in demonstrating your thoughts and feelings.

3.3.2 Organisation and Expression
a) The quality of the structure
This relates to what ACER calls "the shape and form of the piece". If one thinks of a pleasing shape for an essay, it would be an hourglass with a distinct introduction, well-rounded statements for the proposition, a waist indicating change of direction, another well-rounded shape for the counter-argument and a solid conclusion on which the shape rests. The paragraphing for each major point is what gives the essay its structure.

b) The language used

This criterion seeks effectiveness and fluency of language. This means that the words used must be precise and apt in meaning, sentences should be varied in length and in construction and the writing should flow easily. In short, the examiners are looking for the right word in the right place.

3.3.3 Other constraints

Writing Test A must be written within a context of social or cultural relevance. Writing Test B must be reflective and personal but also contain relevance to a social context.

In the next chapter we will explore planning and writing specifically for Writing Test A.

Writing Test A: the socio-cultural essay

The term socio-cultural means issues to do with people in groups (social) and the way in which they live (cultural). Culture includes knowledge, belief, art, morals, law, custom, and any other habits acquired by human beings as members of society. Essays that are based on socio-cultural themes will be about issues to do with human beings in a social and cultural setting.

Examples of current socio-cultural topics in the West are assisted dying, gambling, use and misuse of recreational drugs, racism, obesity, smoking, binge drinking, climate and environmental change and genetically modified farming. Other topics such as immigration, internet control, deforestation, drought or floods and relationships with other countries also offer scope for this type of essay.

Important associated terms are "social costs" and "social benefits". These are not easily quantified but nevertheless are important when considering socio-cultural themes as they are a way of ensuring your essay has included the required socio-cultural element.

Another way of looking at social *costs* is to call costs "effects". We can then see that certain individual behaviours can affect other people although these effects may not always be easily quantified. Think of the pain and suffering and even loss of life experienced by smokers and their families. These are intangible social costs.

Some costs can, however, be quantified. Binge drinking, for example, certainly has quantifiable economic costs such as city centre cleaning, associated health service costs, policing, and legal system involvement but there are also less quantifiable social costs, such as the effects on the family, the association with poverty, performance at work, absenteeism and various forms of violence. You can think of costs as being tangible or intangible.

The social *benefits* of alcohol in low to moderate consumption may be a decreased risk of stroke, occasional increased sense of well-being, some protection against diabetes and a reduction in the risk of heart disease.

This approach can be applied to most forms of human activity.

In addressing Writing Test A it is important to give your view of the topic but also to ensure you consider the socio-cultural perspective through mention of the social *costs* or *benefits* of human activity in your essay.

In this chapter, we are going to apply general principles of essay writing, the GAMSAT criteria for assessment and GAMSAT's additional rules to produce a sample essay. This will help you understand how to plan and write an essay for Writing Test A, the socio-cultural essay. We are going to take animal testing as our theme.

Quotations

I abhor vivisection with my whole soul. All the scientific discoveries stained with innocent blood I count as of no consequence. *Mahatma Gandhi*

The basis of all animal rights should be the Golden Rule: we should treat them as we would wish them to treat us, were any other species in our dominant position. *Christine Stevens*

Many of us would not be able to lead healthy lives were it not for the pharmaceutical companies being able to test their drugs on animals. *Jack Straw*

Vivisection is a social evil because if it advances human knowledge, it does so at the expense of human character. *George Bernard Shaw*

It's vitally important that the research community sends the message that animal research is crucial for medical progress, that it is conducted humanely, and that we work within strict regulations. *Nancy Rothwell*

Step 1 The meaning of the quotation (3 minutes)

These quotations have the common theme of animal testing, some in favour of animal testing and others against. From the quotations, I have derived the title "Does animal testing work?" rather than use one specific quote for our essay.

To ascertain the meaning of our title, we can answer the questions *what, what for, who, why, when.*

The first thing to do is to state what we mean by animal testing, the *what* of the question. Vivisection means to conduct tests on live animals, usually for some scientific purpose. This purpose can be to develop a new drug or to test the toxicity of a chemical, giving the *what for* of the question. *Who does it?* Universities, research laboratories, pharmaceutical companies and farms use animals in research. It is a controversial topic whose opponents argue that animal testing does not work and it should, therefore, be replaced with alternatives.

Step 2 Brainstorming ideas (3 minutes)

Now we need to brainstorm some ideas showing that animal testing does work and others to show it does not. At this point we do not know our conclusion as we have not yet worked through the arguments for and against the proposition that animal testing does not work.

Animal testing does not work *for the proposition*	Animal testing does work *against the proposition*
Animal responses can be different to people's	Developed vaccines e.g. rabies, polio from animal tests
Successful alternatives e.g. include test tube studies on human tissue cultures, statistics and computer models	Antibiotics, HIV drugs, insulin and cancer treatments rely on animal tests. Other testing methods not sufficiently developed
The stress that animals endure in labs can affect experiments, making the results less meaningful	Scientists claim there are no differences in lab animals and humans that cannot be factored into tests

Animals are still used to test items like cleaning products, which benefit mankind less than medicines or surgery	Operations on animals helped to develop organ transplant and open-heart surgery techniques

There are only 25 or so minutes left in which to write this essay so we need to focus on two main points which will give us two in favour of and two against the proposition of the essay title. The most telling ones are the development of drugs and procedures, which can benefit people, and the differences between people and animals that potentially invalidate results of animal tests so those are the ones we are going to focus on in this essay.

Step 3 The introduction (first paragraph)

We need to *explain* the meaning, *expand* this and give an *example*. We also need to state that this is a controversial, frequently debated issue.

"Animal testing refers to experimenting on living, non-human animals for scientific purposes **(explanation)**. Numerous bodies such as universities, drug companies, animal laboratories and commercial enterprises carry out animal testing **(expansion)**. It is used, for example, to test drugs that cannot be tested on people or, in the past, for testing cosmetics **(examples)**. Opposition to animal testing is fierce and one of the arguments commonly used by opponents to animal testing is that it does not work." **(linking sentence)**

Step 4 Second paragraph

Since our last sentence in paragraph 1 refers to opposition to animal testing on the grounds it does not work (*our topic*), we need to raise arguments to support that last sentence. These are going to be to do with the development of drugs without using animals and the differences between animals and human beings which can render the tests meaningless.

"Opponents to animal testing argue that, while drug testing on animals might well produce drugs fit for human use, there are alternatives to animal tests. Basing research on cells in vitro rather than on live animals is one example;

another is better use of statistics such as patient data that monitors the progress of a disease. Yet another is the growing use of new technologies like MRI scanning to help doctors to learn about disease without the need to use animal models."

Step 5 Third paragraph

In the third paragraph we can:

continue with the views of the opponents of animal testing

or

we can counter the claims relating to drug testing and clinical procedures.

In our case, we are going to do the former; we are going to continue with the opponents' perspective. If you do the latter, your fourth paragraph will give a further view from the opponents' bench and a counter-argument to the specific point you raise in the third paragraph.

In our third paragraph, we are going to argue that the differences between animals and human beings can invalidate or reduce the applicability of test results to human beings.

"Another reason given by the opponents of animal testing to show that it does not work is that animals are different from people. By this they mean that animal model reactions to drugs or procedures may not prove to be the same as the reactions of human beings. Examples of this are the recent deaths of people who took an anti-inflammatory drug that had previously been tested on animals. Another example is that of thalidomide, which had also been tested on animals before being given to pregnant women to alleviate symptoms of morning sickness. Opponents doubt that laboratory animals provide accurate models of human diseases and treatments."

Step 6 Fourth paragraph

Now we need to begin our counter-arguments and give the other side's perspective. Remember, two points were raised earlier which we have to tackle. One is the claim that there are good alternatives to animal testing and the other is about the differences between animals and people.

"While it is important to attempt to develop good alternatives to animal testing for human benefit, many scientists feel that animal testing cannot be replaced completely by non-animal methods, particularly in biomedical research. They say the human body is too complex to allow the design of suitable non-animal alternatives and so animal testing must continue. An additional point is that many heart surgery techniques were studied first in dogs before being used in people. Furthermore, neither cells grown outside a body nor computer programs can predict the complex interactions that occur in an entire living system."

Step 7 Fifth paragraph

Here we need an argument to counter the point that animal models may not produce similar results in human beings.

"In addition, researchers can control many aspects of an animal's environment including diet, temperature and lighting, and can factor in compensatory data for the differences. Further, animals are biologically similar to humans in many ways and suffer many of the same health problems. Some species may serve as particularly good models for certain aspects of human health or physiology. Much of what we know about the immune system, for example, has come from studies of mouse models, and much of what we know about the cardiovascular system has come from studies using dogs. Thus, animal testing can prove useful to the development of new drugs despite their different physiology."

Step 8 Sixth and concluding paragraph

In this last paragraph, we must conclude by drawing on ideas expressed in the preceding paragraphs. Our last two paragraphs ended with statements showing that animal testing does work so our conclusion should end by disagreeing with the proposition that animal testing does not work or, better put, that it does indeed work.

"The view that animal testing does not work is not accurate; I have shown that animal testing can produce benefits to humans and that the alternatives have their drawbacks. Nevertheless, if tried and tested alternatives can reduce the numbers of animals used in research and the degree of their suffering, this is obviously desirable. We have a duty to minimise any pain and suffering inflicted upon animals and this means we must continue to find adequate alternatives to animal testing."

The completed essay
"Animal testing does not work"

"Animal testing refers to experimenting on living, non-human animals for scientific purposes. Numerous bodies such as universities, drug companies, animal laboratories and commercial enterprises carry out animal testing. It is used, for example, to test drugs that cannot be tested on people or, in the past, for testing cosmetics. Opposition to animal testing is fierce and one of the arguments commonly used by opponents to animal testing is that it does not work."

"Opponents to animal testing argue that, while drug testing on animals might well produce drugs fit for human use, there are alternatives to animal tests. Basing research on cells in vitro rather than on live animals is one example, another is better use of statistics such as patient data which monitors the progress of a disease. Yet another is the growing use of new technologies like MRI scanning to help doctors to learn about disease without the need to use animal models.

Another reason given by the opponents of animal testing to show that it does not work is that animals are different from people. By this they mean that the animal reactions to drugs and procedures may not prove to be the same as the reactions of human beings. Examples of this are the recent deaths of people who took an anti-inflammatory drug which had previously been tested on animals. Another example is that of thalidomide which had also been tested on animals before being given to pregnant women to alleviate symptoms of morning sickness. Opponents doubt that laboratory animals provide accurate models of human diseases and treatments.

While it is important to attempt to develop good alternatives to animal testing for human benefit, many scientists feel that animal testing cannot be replaced completely by non-animal methods, particularly in biomedical research. They say the human body is too complex to to allow the design of suitable non-animal alternatives and so animal testing must continue. An additional point is that many heart surgery techniques were studied first in dogs before being used in people. Furthermore, neither cells grown outside a body nor computer programs can predict the complex interactions that occur in an entire living system.

In addition, researchers can control many aspects of an animal's environment including diet, temperature, and lighting, and can factor in compensatory data for the differences. Further, animals are biologically similar to humans in many ways and suffer many of the same health problems. Some species may serve as particularly good models for certain aspects of human health or physiology. Much of what we know about the immune system, for example, has come from studies of mouse models, and much of what we know about the cardiovascular system has come from studies using dogs. Thus, animal testing can prove useful to the development of new drugs despite their different physiology.

The view that animal testing does not work is not accurate; I have shown that animal testing can work to produce benefits to humans and that the alternatives have their drawbacks. Nevertheless, if tried and tested alternatives can reduce the numbers of animals used in research and the degree of their suffering, this is obviously desirable. We have a duty to minimise any pain and suffering inflicted upon animals and this means we must continue to find adequate alternatives to animal testing." **(550 words)**

An alternative structure

Instead of arguing two supporting points followed by two paragraphs of counter-arguments, you could show that animal testing does work then follow this by showing that it does not. Your conclusion will be different as you have ended your arguments supporting the proposition; you will end your essay by concluding that, while animal testing is thought to work, there are many potentially reliable alternatives which must be developed.

A further alternative is to raise a point for the proposition then counter it in the next paragraph, then raise the second point for the proposition, then counter it in the next paragraph. This calls for a more neutral conclusion in which you do not take a stand but show that you have dealt with the arguments for and against the topic and that until there are clinically proven alternatives to animal testing, there is no option but for them to continue.

Step 9 Proofread your work

If there is time, read over your work and make any corrections you feel necessary but take care not to ruin your work with wholesale last minute alterations. If you have made a spelling error, delete the word clearly and write the correct one as close to the error as possible. Try to avoid arrows trailing all over the page and do not write at right-angles to the lines.

Writing Test A: Mock Test Essays

The Socio-cultural essay

To recapitulate: the first writing test in GAMSAT is the socio-cultural, more expository essay. See chapter 3 for the detailed criteria. The key point to remember is that the essay should give your view of the topic but also to ensure you consider the socio-cultural perspective through mention of the social *costs* or *benefits* of human activity in your essay.

The essays used in this section were written by candidates who were attending Dr Prep Ltd's preparation courses, using the quotations given below. Each essay is followed by some general remarks and then has a commentary specific to the GAMSAT assessment criteria. The writers have given permission for their essays to be used in this way but the names used are not their real names.

GAMSAT PREPARATION MOCK TEST

WRITTEN COMMUNICATION

Time allowed 30mins

Writing Test A

Consider the following comments and develop a piece of writing in response to one or more of them.

Your writing will be judged on the quality of your response to the theme; how well you organise and present your point of view, and how effectively you express yourself. You will not be judged on the views or attitudes you express.

1) Gambling is as harmless as any other hobby

2) Gambling promises the poor what property performs for the rich--something for nothing. *George Bernard Shaw (1856 - 1950)*

3) Keep flax from fire, youth from gaming *Benjamin Franklin*

4) I used to be a heavy gambler. But now I just make mental bets. That's how I lost my mind. *Steve Allen*

5) Nine gamblers could not feed a single rooster. *Yugoslav proverb*

Writing test A: the socio-cultural essay

It should be clear to you that the overarching topic in writing test A is about gambling and that the views reflected in the quotations are divided with respect to the potential costs and benefits of gambling. Remember that the social costs are not only the costs to an individual but also to society and that you need to include social as well as cultural aspects of the topic in your essay.

It is also worth pointing out that, although you are going to address one or more topics of the five given, you do not need to specify which ones you are responding to. This is good as it means you can take either a general or a more specific approach to the overarching theme. You can give a title to your essay if you wish; it can help you to focus on the brief but there are no additional marks for doing so.

What would be expected in a good response to this writing test A?

One would expect to see some, if not all of, the following points depending on the quotation.

- a cogent introduction e.g. current relevance
- at least two points in favour and two against gambling
- explanations and supporting examples
- some mention of the potential costs to society such as
  - poverty
  - break up of families
  - treatment of addiction
- the potential benefits (taxation, employment)
- some concluding remarks based on the preceding paragraphs.

Since the quotations on gambling have much the same theme, that gambling involves almost certain loss, the structure above can easily be adapted to suit any essay on gambling. In other words, the outline above is generic to the subject of gambling. This is likely to be true for most socio-cultural essays so it is important that you identify the overarching theme of all the quotations before you develop your structure.

The essays discussed here have been assessed using the mark scheme below, using a weighting of 60% towards the thought and content and 40% assigned to organisation and expression. The mark scheme has been derived from the GAMSAT published criteria, and will not be identical to that used by ACER themselves.

GAMSAT SOCIO-CULTURAL ESSAY MARK SCHEME	
Thought and content 60 marks (10 marks for each point)	
The thoughts & feelings offered	• fully relevant to brief
	• insightful
	• assertions explained
	• assertions exemplified
What is made of the brief	• individual not stock answer
	• coherent perspective
Organisation and expression 40 marks (5 for each point)	
The quality of the structure	• sufficient coverage of topic
	• appropriate style for theme
	• coherence within paragraphs
	• paragraphs connected to each other
	• conclusion based on paragraphs
The quality of the language	• well-selected vocabulary
	• creative sentence structure
	• appropriate language use

Overall grade as %					
Below 40%	40 -49	50 -55	56 - 59	60 -69	70 & above
Thought and content (quality of what is said) the kinds of thought and feeling offered in response to the brief					
irrelevant to brief unintelligent meaningless	misinterpreted prompt naïve	inconsistent relationship to brief	relates to all main themes of the brief	relates to all main themes insightful on some	relates to all main themes insightful on many fronts
Thought and content (quality of what is said) what is made of and developed from the brief					
no recognisable viewpoint	lack of clarity confusing simplistic treatment	assertions without evidence	viewpoint with evidence expected answer	cohesive viewpoint 'individual' answer	integrates insights apt evidence well developed perspective
Organisation and expression (the quality of the structure) the shape and form of the piece (para = paragraph)					
incoherent too brief for productive response	wrong genre or style for the brief	poorly organised lack of coherence within paragraphs	themes develop within paragraphs paragraphs poorly connected	paragraph themes directed toward viewpoint paragraphs well constructed	cohesive overall between and within paragraphs
Organisation and expression (the quality of the language used) the effectiveness and fluency of language					
unacceptable level of language skills uses slang and informal language	limited vocabulary multiple errors in language consistently poor grammar	poor use of English some errors	competent use of language and sentence structures	well-selected vocabulary varied sentence structure	exceptional use of vocabulary creative variations in sentence structure

How to use the timed mock essays

1. Read through the first essay.

2. Make appropriate comments in the text or elsewhere according to the scheme above.

3. Using the mark scheme above allocate marks for each point.

4. Add the two marks together for the overall percentage.

5. Read the commentary at the end of each essay and decide if you agree with the marks awarded.

6. Repeat in turn for each essay in this chapter.

7. You can use this model to mark your own practice essays.

James Gambling promises the poor what property performs for the rich- something for nothing. *George Bernard Shaw*

$\frac{1}{2}$ 59

James p.1

'Gambling promises the poor what property performs for the rich -- something for nothing' - George Bernard Shaw

In making this statement, Shaw is asserting that, for the poorer segments of society, who do not have significant amounts of capital or property, gambling is the only way they can make money without doing anything. The implication is that this is an empty promise however, as he contrasts the 'promise' with what property 'performs'. Another message somewhat implicit is that the rich do not necessarily deserve this 'something for nothing'. This statement still has resonance today; the majority of people who play the national lottery are from lower socioeconomic groups.

Furthermore, the money raised from the lottery goes on to fund arts and theatre programs that are more frequently attended by those from higher income groups; in effect, a tax on the poor. As house prices rise, and the relative distribution of wealth in our society becomes more unequal over time (as is occurring now), the 'promise' of gambling will become more seductive. Already, there is a greater risk of gambling addiction amongst lower income groups and the consequences for those without a safety net of savings or property can be much greater than for those who have things; thus, the poor have less to lose. It is this injustice that Shaw seeks to highlight.

However, perhaps gambling can be viewed as a little harmless fun? People do win the lottery, and it can change their lives, for example. Also the rich gamble as well, in stocks and shares and on the assumption that house prices will rise, not fall.* As the Lloyds names found out, even if you have a lot, you can still lose it all in an

$\frac{2}{2}$ 60

[handwritten essay text, partially legible:]

The long of the instant, the fact that many of them managed to get a lot of their money back would not, one suspects, be lost on Shaw. Certainly, the Lloyds names seem to have been more successful in retaining their assets than the victims of the Fanpak collapse or those who have lost money in the various pension fund debacles of recent years.

In conclusion, it is hard, even now, not to argue with Shaw's point. The poor gamble because it is their only hope, whilst the rich are more insulated by their wealth, which in turn generates more wealth, or 'something for nothing.'

Footnote (sorry!)

* Also, the money they have may well have been earnt by dint of hard work and dedication.

General commentary on James' essay

James has tackled the most difficult of the quotations as it deals with two issues, that of getting something for nothing and the differing approaches taken by rich and poor. He makes an excellent start by fully explaining his introductory remarks and his assertions are exemplified throughout, leading the reader to an informed and considered conclusion.

His footnote is redundant and should have been omitted.

James' examples are current and apt, his use of language is appropriate to the theme.

His handwriting makes the essay less pleasant to read than one would wish but does not detract greatly from the meaning. This is his greatest weakness.

Specific commentary
Thought and content (quality of thought and feelings)
Relevance to brief
Insightful

James's introduction shows a clear grasp of the meaning of the quotation. He also gives a secondary interpretation, the inference that Shaw does not approve of the role of property in contributing to the wealth of rich people. James contrasts the word 'promise' with 'perform' and suggests the former is empty when applied to gambling by poor people. James, thus, demonstrates insight in his introduction.

He might have included some explanation of the resonance of property ownership for wealthy people today in the same way as he explains the contribution to the national lottery by poorer people.

Thought and content (what is made of and developed from the task)
Assertions exemplified
Assertions backed up with evidence
Individual answer rather than expected answer
Coherent perspective

James continues his theme in paragraph two by explaining how although people from poorer backgrounds contribute most to the national lottery, they may not benefit from some of the arts and theatre projects funded by the lottery. He also shows how this group has more to lose from gambling as they have no access to spare wealth or property. The concept of injustice is raised explicitly to illustrate the meaning of Shaw's quotation.

In paragraph three we see James attempt to give some balance to the argument by suggesting that gambling might be harmless but he cannot maintain this position for long and shows how, even though the rich may lose assets, their wealth allows them to recover faster than poorer people and contrasts the Lloyds names collapse with that of Farepak in which thousands of people lost their Christmas savings.

Note that the Farepak scheme could not be called gambling, neither can investment in a pension scheme. James might have been better off using examples focussed on gambling although the purpose of these was to compare the speed of recovery from disaster available to wealthy people to that available to the poor.

James' conclusion supports Shaw's initial assertion despite his attempt to find a counter argument; it is clear what James' views on gambling are with respect to the rich and poor.

James could have mentioned the connection between wealth and property in the context of gambling on future price rises and the negative equity experienced by many in the 1980s. This would add a little more balance by showing that property does not always perform favourably as an investment.

He does not become tempted to discuss the harm caused by gambling but sticks to his brief. James does allow himself a viewpoint by choosing some specific examples and manages to induce some sympathy among his readers for people who lose money through gambling although our sympathy is less towards the rich than the poor.

Organisation and expression
Structure (shape and form)
sufficient coverage of topic
coherence within paragraphs
paragraphs connected to each other
paragraphs develop theme
conclusion derived from paragraphs

The essay allows sufficient coverage of the topic; each paragraph contains a single thought and is internally consistent. The paragraphs connect to each other with linking words such as 'furthermore', 'however' and 'in conclusion'. Each paragraph develops the theme set out in the quotation so that the conclusion neatly turns back to Shaw's quotation.

Organisation and expression
Effectiveness and fluency of language
good range of vocabulary
appropriate use of language
conventional grammar

James' use of language is fluent with a mature vocabulary and varied sentence structure. His writing is grammatically correct and free of spelling errors.

James' handwriting makes more work for the examiner than one would like. I would advise him to practise writing several essays by hand before the test date. I have deducted some marks in the organisation and expression section to compensate for the extra effort I had to make to read his handwriting!

Marks out of 60

Thought and content

Relevance to brief	8/10
Insightful	7/10
Assertions explained	8/10
Assertions exemplified	9/10
Individual answer	9/10
Coherent perspective	9/10
TOTAL	**50/60**

Organisation and expression

Coverage of topic	4/5
Coherence of paragraphs	4/5
Paragraphs connected	4/5
Paragraphs develop theme	4/5
Conclusion from paragraphs	5/5
Good range of vocabulary	5/5
Appropriate use of language	4/5
Conventional grammar	5/5
TOTAL	**35/40**

Overall total	**85%**

Amy Gambling promises the poor what property performs for the rich - something for nothing. *George Bernard Shaw*

TEST A. TOPIC 2).   PAGE 1.   93

PLAN.
                                              property
    1. Intro- define gambling & ~~hoer hobby~~ e.g's
    2. For - advantages
    3. Against - disadvantages.
    4. Conc^n - summarise.

Introduction
    ~~The term Gambling sug relate means~~ This
quote ~~suggest~~ by George Bernard Shaw suggests that
Gambling itself does not cost anything, but the outcomes
can reap huge rewards, that money could have bought. It
also implies that property is a valuable asset to affluent
people who feel they have not paid anything. However, to
say gambling promises, is slightly ambiguous, I feel, as
nothing can be promised or guaranteed in this world,
~~&~~ and the term gambling is certainly a contradiction to
the term promises. To take a gamble is to take a
chance, not ~~~~ confirm an outcome.
    Reasons why this statement may be true, are in
cases such as that of property investors. Although 'something
can't come out of nothing, these such people can put in
a significantly small sum of money (which may seem like
nothing to them), and get a huge reward out of it, which
will mean something, if not to them, then definitely to
others, such as the poor, who gamble nothing to get
something. In addition, a pauper ~~~~ who is a beginner at
gambling may have a lucky day, ~~so~~ and get something
out of it.
    However, this statement can also be construed as a
slight fabrication. Everyday people take a gamble, which
can be as fundamental as the attire you wear, to something
more significant and important, such as the choice you
make which may affect those around you - for example
if you were a Doctor. The contradiction in this
comment is the word promises. To say a promise is as
good as saying an oath - ~~somett~~ something you believe

Amy p2   TEST A. TOPIC 2). contd.   PAGE 2.

in, something you can guarantee. Gambling is all about taking risks, playing your chances, and hoping for the best. If a less wealthy person feels that gambling his earnings will promise him twice as much money, he may take this risk and gamble, at the price of what he owes. However, there is no promise that, once he has gambled (in this case, conventional gambling games such as poker), he will reap twice of what his original earnings were. In this case, he has not got something for nothing, but instead the very opposite. He has put something in (in the hope to get something more out), but infact, he has now ended up with nothing.

George Bernard Shaw's statement could insinuate "poor" as those who lack the knowledge, not necessarily the monetary & possessions. An example could be a student who has taken a chance to apply to Medical School. This may not have come at a cost and so therefore they have put nothing in, but the outcome is not promised, and they may not get something out of it, because the competition may have been just too tough, hence they may have missed out on a possible place at medical school.

Conclusion
     This comment could be taken literally, and be applied to situations of money, and it can also be read in the context of the subtext, that is anything can come out of putting nothing in.
     However, I feel that although this statement can be applied to situations (as above), it is generally a false prediction, and more often than not, not give you something for nothing.

General commentary on Amy's essay

Amy's topic is the same as the previous writer's but her approach is quite different and it is, at times, difficult to follow her train of thought. This essay demonstrates how crucial it is to get the interpretation of the brief correct from the outset. Amy's introduction gropes towards an understanding of the quotation, she has understood that for a small stake large riches can be won but has missed Shaw's cynicism about the role of property in bolstering the wealth of the already well-off and the greed of both rich and poor in desiring wealth for no effort. Amy makes too much of the word 'promise' and tries to hang the rest of the essay on this word rather than mentioning the delusions of believing such promises. She fails to mention the wider social costs of gambling as she goes off the track by discussing gambling on clothes or choice of a career, which is irrelevant to Shaw's quote and is hardly a gamble in the accepted use of the term. She needs to stick to real gambling, the hope of gain in return for some monetary risk. Then she can conclude with the social costs of gambling such as destitution and the destruction of family life. Overall, this is a confused and confusing essay in which the reader has to try to disentangle the threads of her thinking. Strangely enough, the crossing out does not distract the reader very much.

Specific commentary
Thought and content (quality of thought and feelings)
Relevance to brief
Insightful

Amy shows a partial understanding of the brief and demonstrates some insight into the similarities posed between the two groups of people in the quotation. She takes rather a long time to make a simple point which is best expressed in the last line of her first paragraph.

Thought and content (what is made of and developed from the task)
Assertions exemplified
Assertions backed up with evidence
Individual answer rather than expected answer
Coherent perspective

Amy does try to explain her assertions in her first and second paragraphs but her thinking is muddled and does not help to enlighten the reader further. She could have explained more clearly the risk poor people are willing to take in the hope of gain and show that rich people do not need to do this as they have assets such as property whose value can grow without their making much effort. The thinking is not coherent; she flounders towards clarifying her thoughts. She states that poor people gamble 'nothing' in order to gain 'something'. This is clearly not the case as 'something' however small, has to be staked on a possible win.

Amy does provide examples for her assertions although some of these such as 'gambling ' on choice of clothing or career where the risk is not the same as staking a bet against almost certain financial loss are irrelevant. In addition, the motivation to take that risk is dissimilar. The last sentence of paragraph one is the best of the paragraph and could have been used as her opening statement.

Organisation and expression
Structure (shape and form)
Sufficient coverage of topic
Coherence within paragraphs
Paragraphs connected to each other
Paragraphs develop theme
Conclusion based on paragraphs

Generally, Amy's structure is sound. She uses paragraphs effectively, it is just that her thoughts ramble and are not always relevant to the topic. Some of the paragraphs contain too many thoughts, for example in paragraph three, where there is too much hanging on the word, 'promise'. The theme is not developed much beyond the testing her ideas against the notion of promise. The conclusion is not related to the preceding paragraphs but introduces a new idea in the first sentence. This is never a good idea: the conclusion must sum up the thoughts so far and must not bring up new ideas because there is no time to deal with them.

Organisation and expression
Effectiveness and fluency of language
Good range of vocabulary
Appropriate use of language
Conventional grammar

Amy's use of language is generally sound. There are some lapses in expression such as 'slight fabrication'. Fabrication is the wrong word here and 'slight' is the wrong adjective to describe it. She may mean that the quotation is simplistic or is an overstatement, we cannot tell for sure, but she means that she does not agree with the quotation. She would have been better off saying this bluntly and then justifying what she means. Amy could improve her language by using shorter sentences and simpler vocabulary. As it is, her vocabulary and sentence structure is varied but one of her flaws is the wrong choice of word such as 'insinuate' in paragraph four when 'imply' might be a better word in this context.

Marks out of 60

Thought and content

Relevance to brief	6/10
Insightful	5/10
Assertions explained	6/10
Assertions exemplified	6/10
Individual answer	5/10
Coherent perspective	5/10
TOTAL	**33/60**

Organisation and expression

Coverage of topic	3/5
Coherence of paragraphs	2/5
Paragraphs connected	3/5
Paragraphs develop theme	2/5
Conclusion from paragraphs	1/5
Good range of vocabulary	3/5
Appropriate use of language	3/5
Conventional grammar	3/5
TOTAL	**20/40**

Overall total	**53%**

Nadine *Gambling, good or bad?*

PAGE ①

Nadine p1

ESSAY A (1)   GAMBLING : GOOD OR BAD?

THIS QUOTE IMPLIES THAT GAMBLING IS A PLEASURABLE AND FUN PURSUIT AND ~~THE GAMBLING~~ HAS NO DAMAGING CONSEQUENCES AND THEREFORE ~~CAN BE COMPARED WITH OR~~ IS SIMILAR TO OTHER HOBBIES SUCH AS GOING TO THE PUB OR SOCIALISING WITH FRIENDS. ~~EVEN~~ GAMBLING CAN FORM PART OF MEETING UP WITH FRIENDS ~~AND IS~~ AND IS, THEREFORE, VIEWED AS A SOCIABLE HOBBY. AN EXAMPLE IS THE NATIONAL LOTTERY, WHICH ALSO BRINGS A SENSE OF CAMARADERIE AS MANY COME TOGETHER TO FORM SYNDICATES AND IT GIVES THEM A COMMON GROUND WITH PEOPLE THEY MAY NEVER HAVE SOCIALISED WITH.

OTHER HARMLESS ATTRIBUTES OF GAMBLING IS THE FACT THAT IT CAN GIVE PEOPLE SOME HOPE THAT THEIR LIFE CAN CHANGE AND, SO HELPS PEOPLE TO REMAIN POSITIVE. GAMBLING, ~~CAN HELP FINANCE~~ FURTHERMORE, EVENTS LIKE THE NATIONAL LOTTERY HELP TO IMPROVE OUR COMMUNITIES BY PROVIDING GRANTS FOR A NUMBER OF SMALL PROJECTS ACROSS THE U.K SUCH AS GARDENING FOR THE DISABLED AND THE RESTORATION OF A NUMBER OF LEISURE PARKS.

HOWEVER, GAMBLING IS NOT WITHOUT ITS PROBLEMS. ~~A~~ SMALL FLUTTERS CAN END UP RESULTING IN AN ADDICTION TO GAMBLING, WHICH HAS BEEN EVIDENCED BY STATISTICS ~~AND . OF~~ THE NATIONAL LOTTERY HAS BEEN GLAMOURISED ~~AND~~ HAS ENCOURAGED THE TYPE OF LIFESTYLE THAT MANY ASPIRE TO. ~~IN A BID~~ TO WIN THIS LIFE OF LUXURY, MANY ARE SPENDING MORE THAN THEY COULD POSSIBLY AFFORD. THIS HAS ~~ALSO~~ RESULTED IN DEBTS ACCUMULATING, AND THE NEED TO TAKE OUT LOANS TO COVER THE DEBT. EVENTUALLY, INDIVIDUALS FIND THAT THEY ARE LOSING THE BATTLE ~~AND SEEKING~~ AND SEEK MORE LOANS TO COVER THE DEBT. THE INDIVIDUAL'S HEALTH IS OFTEN AT RISK AS A RESULT OF THIS

PAGE (2)

Nadine p2

ESSAY A (1)

STRESS. MANY HAVE PRESENTED WITH HIGH BLOOD
PRESSURE ~~strikethrough~~ AS WELL AS
BEING UNABLE TO SLEEP. MOUNTING DEBTS CAN
LEAVE INDIVIDUALS FEELING $ DESPONDENT AND EVEN
SUICIDAL. THUS THERE IS A GREAT ETHICAL CONCERN WITH
                                    RELATED TO GAMBLING.

GAMBLING IS HARMLESS IN SMALL DOSES AND WHERE
THERE IS A VERY SMALL RISK. HOWEVER, WEAKNESSES
OF INDIVIDUALS COUPLED WITH THE MILLIONAIRES'
LIFESTYLE THAT ARE ~~strikethrough~~ WELL DOCUMENTED AND
PUBLICISED BY MOVIE STARS CAN MAKE GAMBLING
VERY DIFFICULT TO RESIST. PEOPLE ALSO INDULGE
IN GAMBLING TO ~~strikethrough~~ BLOCK OUT ~~strikethrough~~ THE WORRIES ~~strikethrough~~
TO IN THEIR LIFES AND THUS IT IS A FORM OF
'ESCAPISM'. ~~strikethrough~~

                                    EMERGED
A NUMBER OF PRESSURE GROUPS HAS ~~strikethrough~~ AS
A RESULT IN THE SURGE OF GAMBLING AND
THE DEVASTATING IMPACT IT HAS HAD ON FAMILIES.
THIS WOULD SUGGEST THAT GAMBLING REALLY IS
SEEN AS A PROBLEM RATHER THAN A HARMLESS
HOBBY. GAMBLING NEEDS TO BE REGULATED MORE
~~THAN~~ THOROUGHLY BY THE GOVERNMENT AND ITS ~~EFFECT~~
CONSEQUENCES ~~strikethrough~~ SHOULD BE WELL-PUBLICISED
IF WE WISH FOR IT TO REMAIN HARMLESS.

General commentary on Nadine's essay

The things that strike the reader at first sight are that the essay contains messy alterations and is written entirely in unconnected block letters. The messiness distracts the reader's attention from the meaning of the words, so Nadine needs to think first and then write. The unconnected capital letters are unusual but it is better to use block letters if your cursive (joined-up or running) handwriting is untidy.

Her introduction demonstrates she has a good grasp of the meaning of the quotation, namely that gambling is as harmless as any other hobby. We would expect to see some arguments for and against gambling. If this were to be an excellent essay, we would also expect to see something about the effects of any hobby taken to extremes. Nadine gives the conventional arguments for and against gambling and uses several examples to support her argument. However, she repeats herself in the penultimate paragraph and this wastes both her and the reader's time. She could instead have compared gambling to other hobbies or given examples of small-time gambling such as bingo which is not necessarily harmful.

Nadine demonstrates clearly how gambling can be harmful although she could give more emphasis to the social costs to families, the benefit system and the health service. Families suffer not only through depleted financial resources but also through the lack of attention paid to family life by gamblers.

Specific commentary
Thought and content (quality of thought and feelings)
Relevance to brief
Insightful

Nadine's opening sets out clearly the essay that follows. Her title shows the simplicity of her approach, which is followed through in the essay itself. She gives an apt example to illustrate the point made in the second sentence. The introduction is relevant to the brief and shows some insight into one aspect of gambling, the social nature of the activity although she does not mention on-line or other solitary aspects of gambling. She does not allude to the costs of gambling in her introduction but these are raised in subsequent paragraphs.

Thought and content (what is made of and developed from the task)
Assertions exemplified
Assertions backed up with evidence
Individual answer rather than expected answer
Coherent perspective

The assertions made are backed up by examples and references to the deleterious effects on personal health of uncontrolled gambling. Nadine makes an unsubstantiated reference to statistics on gambling as an addiction (paragraph three), which might have been better expressed as a possibility rather than as a fact. Her response is conventional but thorough for all that. Her perspective is coherent throughout, apart from the repetitious argument in the fourth paragraph. She has given a good example of the contentious nature of gambling through her use of the example of pressure groups to support gamblers. Nadine could have mentioned the profit to be made from gambling, in particular the tax revenues available to governments and, in this context, the proposals to set up super casinos in the UK. Her mention of the ethical concerns about gambling is a useful one.

Organisation and expression
Structure (shape and form)
Sufficient coverage of topic
Coherence within paragraphs
Paragraphs connected to each other
Paragraphs develop theme
Conclusion based on paragraphs

The shape of this essay is generally well balanced. The topic has enough coverage to convince the reader of her arguments for and against gambling; the paragraphs are internally consistent and there are links between paragraphs. Each paragraph (bar the fourth) takes the main point forward, leading to the only possible conclusion. She has added a good point about the need to regulate gambling more effectively.

Organisation and expression
Effectiveness and fluency of language
Good range of vocabulary
Appropriate use of language
Conventional grammar

Nadine's use of language is generally good. She uses one word which is out of place in formal writing, the use of the word 'fun' as an adjective. It is a colloquial usage and merely repeats her earlier word, 'pleasurable', adding nothing to her meaning. Her vocabulary, although simple, is adequate to her task and her grammar is accurate.

Marks out of 60
Thought and content

Relevance to brief	8/10
Insightful	6/10
Assertions explained	7/10
Assertions exemplified	6/10
Individual answer	6/10
Coherent perspective	8/10
TOTAL	**41/60**

Organisation and expression

Coverage of topic	4/5
Coherence of paragraphs	4/5
Paragraphs connected	5/5
Paragraphs develop theme	5/5
Conclusion from paragraphs	5/5
Good range of vocabulary	3/5
Appropriate use of language	4/5
Conventional grammar	5/5
TOTAL	**35/40**

Overall total	**76**%

Writing Test B: the personal, social or reflective essay

Before reading this chapter, please ensure you are familiar with the meaning of the assessment criteria given in Chapter 3.

As we did in Chapter 4, in this chapter, we are going to apply general principles of essay writing, the GAMSAT criteria for assessment and additional rules to produce a sample essay. This will help you understand how to plan and write an essay for Writing Test B, the personal, social or reflective essay. We are going to take forgiveness as our theme.

The topics for this task require a more personal response but still with a social dimension. A good approach is to reflect on an issue of meaning in your life that has relevance to the topic set. Bear in mind that the essay must also contain some socio-cultural comment.

The important person in this essay is you, the writer, and so the word "I" can be used. A common error is to treat this type of essay as expository and write in an impersonal, objective way to produce an essay which is neither reflective nor personal. Not only is it acceptable to use "I" in the personal essay, it is advisable.

In order to reflect on a theme, you require a relevant experience. The experience will have circumstances, an event, consequences and feelings that can be described to the reader. What follows, then, is an analysis of the experience and particularly the consequences to you and others. Most important is the lesson learned and the changes you have made as a result. You can describe how you have applied the lesson to your life and the effects of this on other people, for example, in the workplace, on your family and friends or in some other social setting. You are firmly at the centre of this essay whether your experience is invented or real.

71

The process looks like this:

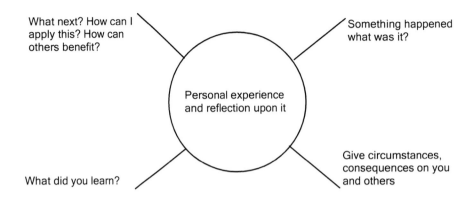

Examples of suitable topics for reflection are perseverance and other human "virtues", accidents and mistakes, travel, study, ambition and zeal. There are, of course, many, many others as online quotation websites will show.

Quotations

It is easier to forgive an enemy than to forgive a friend. *William Blake*

The weak can never forgive. Forgiveness is the attribute of the strong. *Mahatma Gandhi*

Forgiveness is the oil of relationships.

To forgive all is as inhuman as to forgive none. *Seneca*

Forgive all who have offended you, not for them, but for yourself. *Harriet Nelson*

Step 1 The meaning of the quotation (3 minutes)

The general theme is forgiveness and you have been provided with a number of different suggestions - that it is easier to forgive people you do not like than those you do; that strong people forgive others; that forgiveness is essential to friendship; that it is not possible to forgive everyone or everything; that to forgive benefits the forgiver.

You may use to one or more quotes depending on which ones you feel you can best respond to or you may find it easier to write generally on the theme of forgiveness from a personal perspective. In any event, you need to establish the meaning of the term or act as it will apply in your essay. Remember that the meaning can be derived through the questions *what, what for, who,* and we can add *to whom,* and *in what circumstances.*

The meaning of forgiveness

Forgiveness is an emotional process whereby a person ceases to feel anger or resentment against another for an act or offence. There may be some other emotion such as compassion or tolerance involved. Forgiveness may be granted without punishment, compensation or other penalty or without the knowledge of the forgiven person. The practice of forgiveness is taught by most major religions, some of these teachings providing an underlying basis for many modern day traditions and practices of forgiveness. The ability to forgive may be desirable but is easier said than done.

We are going to use the quotations to write on the theme of "Forgive and forget?" The question mark indicates that we are not sure whether it is always possible to forgive as well as forget. We are going to describe an experience, reflect on it, draw some lessons and say how we have applied them.

Step 2 Brainstorming ideas (3-5 minutes)

Example of poor company practices

Effects on me

My response

Lessons

Practical and how socially relevant

Conclusion

Step 3 The introduction (first paragraph)

We are going to say what we mean by the title, something about the meaning of forgiveness and something general about the benefits of forgiveness and the harm than occurs when resentment is harboured. We might mention how we are going to tackle this essay but on the other hand time is short so we will probably just get stuck in and write.

"Forgiveness suggests excusing an offence and is commonly introduced with the words, "I'm sorry." Forgiveness means to let go of the resentment caused by an act or the behaviour of a person. True forgiveness means resolving anger and replacing it with compassion or some other less unpleasant emotion. Sometimes, however, forgiveness is not possible as I found during an experience of working abroad."

The scene is set, definitions given and the scope of the essay laid out.

Step 4 Second paragraph

In this paragraph, we are going to describe the experience of poor company practice during a year spent working abroad. This answers *'what happened?'*

"I spent my gap year in Japan teaching at an English language school. I left the UK with high expectations of life in a new culture, of teaching adults and experiencing life in Tokyo, where I had specifically asked to be sent. Conditions were attached to my stay such as the refund of the airfare, my payment for housing and furniture. There would be little money left once the various payments were made but worse was to follow. My accommodation was an hour's travel out of Tokyo, my housing was poor, I had to pay rent for bedding

and I was given young children to teach. I was not paid for my travelling between schools. I could not reclaim my airfare until I had worked for a year so I could not leave the school without sacrificing the money that I had borrowed from my parents. I felt outraged that I had been so badly exploited and let down. Eventually I set up a branch of a trade union in my school and held regular staff meetings fuelled largely by my burning resentment. Little changed however."

Step 5 Third paragraph
This paragraph finishes off the description of the experience.

"After a year of living with this constant seething anger, I realised I was harming myself and decided to leave before the full term of my contract expired. There was little point in trying to improve the working terms and conditions for colleagues since the real culprits, the school's owners, were impervious to my efforts. I concluded that it was not realistic to continue to struggle. I left the school and my apartment with great relief and thought nothing more of the corruption of the school and its owners."

Step 6 Fourth paragraph
Now we move into the analysis phase, explaining the lessons learned and relating them to the title.

"From this experience I learned that holding on to anger is harmful. It hurt me to stay resentful as it meant I could not enjoy my experiences of living in a new city. My time and energy was spent organising meetings or thinking about the latest indignity I was going to fight. Although I have largely forgotten those days, I do not think that even now, several years on, I am able to forgive the school for the shoddy way they treated their staff. I may have forgotten the experience but the lessons I learned have remained."

Step 7 Fifth paragraph.

Now we need to tie all the thinking together and mention any long-lasting lessons which we have used or can use in a new social setting.

"Since my return to the UK, I carefully check the terms and conditions of all contracts I am offered, whether for employment or otherwise and have told my friends to do the same. Currently, I ensure my team have good working conditions. While the anger about my experience has dissipated, I can use the lessons to prevent the exploitation of other people. I also warn friends about teaching English with this particular firm. To do all these things has helped me to let go of the anger. But I have neither forgiven the school nor wholly forgotten my experiences in it."

Step 8 Concluding paragraph

We need to return to the introduction and check whether we have covered all the ideas raised in it. We will write a paragraph that relates to the introduction and come to a view about what made it impossible to forgive.

"From this particular experience I see that it is not always possible to forgive even if it is possible to forget unpleasant circumstances such as betrayal of my expectations of good company practice. It was a bitter experience but the lessons I learned can be applied to other situations. On reflection, I think the exploitation by my employer was the chief source of anger and it is this I have not been able to forgive. Perhaps betrayal is the hardest for people to forgive whether by an employer, friends or family. It is not a lapse or an error but a deliberate act which makes true forgiveness impossible for some."

The completed essay
"Forgive and forget?"

Forgiveness suggests excusing an offence and is commonly introduced with the words, "I'm sorry." Forgiveness means to let go of the resentment caused by an act or the behaviour of a person. True forgiveness means resolving anger and replacing it with compassion or some other less unpleasant emotion. Sometimes, however, forgiveness is not possible as I found during an experience of working abroad.

I spent my gap year in Japan teaching at an English language school. I left the UK with high expectations of life in a new culture, of teaching adults, and experiencing life in Tokyo where I had specifically asked to be sent. Conditions were attached to my stay such as the refund of the airfare, my payment for housing and furniture. There would be little money left once various payments were made but worse was to follow. My accommodation was an hour's travel out of Tokyo, my housing was poor, I had to pay rent for bedding, and I was given young children to teach. I was not paid for my travelling between schools, I could not reclaim my airfare until I had worked a year so I could not leave the school without sacrificing the money that I had borrowed from my parents. I felt outraged that I had been so badly exploited and let down. Eventually I set up a branch of a trade union in my school and held regular staff meetings fuelled largely by my burning resentment. Little changed however.

After a year of living with this constant seething anger, I realised I was harming myself and decided to leave before the full term of my contract expired. There was little point in trying to improve the working terms and conditions for colleagues since the real culprits, the school's owners, were impervious to my efforts. I concluded that it was not realistic to continue to struggle. I left the school and my apartment with great relief and thought nothing more of the corruption of the school and its owners.

From this experience I learned that holding on to anger is harmful. It hurt me to stay resentful as it meant I could not enjoy my experiences of living in a new city. My time and energy was spent organising meetings or thinking about the latest indignity I was going to fight. Although I have largely forgotten those days, I do not think even now, several years on, I am able to forgive the school for the shoddy way they treated their staff. I may have forgotten the experience but the lessons I learned have remained.

Since my return to the UK, I carefully check the terms and conditions of all contracts I am offered, whether for employment or otherwise and have told my friends to do the same. Currently, I ensure my team have good working conditions. While the anger about my experience has dissipated, I can use the lessons to prevent the exploitation of other people. I also warn friends about teaching English with this particular firm. To do all these things has helped me to let go of the anger. But I have neither forgiven the school nor wholly forgotten my experiences in it.

From this particular experience I see that it is not always possible to forgive even if it is possible to forget unpleasant circumstances such as betrayal of my expectations of good company practice. It was a bitter experience but the lessons I learned can be applied to other situations. On reflection, I think the exploitation by my employer was the chief source of anger and it is this I have not been able to forgive. Perhaps betrayal is the hardest for people to forgive whether by an employer, friends or family. It is not a lapse or an error but a deliberate act which makes true forgiveness impossible for some. (644 words)

Writing Test B: Mock Test Essays

The personal essay

To recapitulate: the second writing test in GAMSAT is the personal, more reflective essay. See chapter 3 for the detailed criteria. The key point to remember is that the essay should be about your experience, whether imaginary or real. You must show how your views or your life were changed by your experiences and how you have used or can use these changed attitudes in your life.

The essays used in this section were written as part of preparing for GAMSAT using the quotations given below. Each essay is followed by some general remarks and then has a commentary specific to the GAMSAT assessment criteria. The writers have given permission for their essays to be used in this way but the names used are not their real names.

GAMSAT PREPARATION MOCK TEST

WRITTEN COMMUNICATION

Time allowed 30mins

Writing Test B

Consider the following comments and develop a piece of writing in response to one or more of them.

Your writing will be judged on the quality of your response to the theme; how well you organise and present your point of view, and how effectively you express yourself. You will not be judged on the views or attitudes you express.

1) Certainly, travel is more than the seeing of sights; it is a change that goes on, deep and permanent, in the ideas of living. *Miriam Beard*

2) Travel broadens the mind.

3) The traveller sees what he sees, the tourist sees what he has come to see. *GK Chesterton*

4) All travel has its advantages. If the traveller visits better countries, he may learn to improve his own; and if fortune carries him to worse, he may learn to enjoy his own. **Dr Johnson**

5) See one promontory, one mountain, one sea, one river, and see all. *Socrates*

It is evident from the quotations in test B, that the theme here is travel, which in this case can also imply a personal journey. Because there is a social element to the topic, you must mention how your experiences of travel can affect others in your own society or show you can use your experiences in a positive manner.

Quotations 1, 2, and 4 imply that to travel is beneficial to the traveller whatever the experiences. Quotations 1 and 2 are similar in theme implying that long-lasting change to the individual occurs as a result of travel. Quotation 4 suggests that travel allows us to use the experience to improve or enjoy our own country.

Quotation 3 implies that what is experienced depends on the traveller's attitude to travel and whether they are sightseers or sojourners observing a society.

In quotation 5, Socrates suggests that all physical landmarks are the same. This quotation could be taken to mean that travel is a waste of time; once one has seen a different place, there is no point in further travel. On the other hand, it could mean that we should look beyond physical sights when we travel or it could mean that we need to look beyond travel (or indeed other activities or pursuits) for meaning and purpose in our lives. It is a difficult topic as there are so many possible interpretations but it also offers scope for a discussion on the benefits or otherwise of chasing dreams.

What can be expected in a good response to quotations 1 and 2

1) *Certainly, travel is more than the seeing of sights; it is a change that goes on, deep and permanent, in the ideas of living.* **Miriam Beard**

2) *Travel broadens the mind.*

1) An introduction which shows your views about something before your journey
2) Brief example of the experience
    country
    your age at the time (only if relevant)
    purpose of the trip
    duration
3) Lessons learned from the experience
4) Benefits of your travel to you
5) Use of this experience to benefit others
6) Conclusion based on the preceding paragraphs

What can be expected in a good response to quotation 3

3) *The traveller sees what he sees, the tourist sees what he has come to see.*
Chesterton

1) Introduction: a statement explaining the quotation
2) Explanation of the difference between a traveller and a tourist
    i) Flexible observer of and participant in the host society
    ii) Sightseer, possible fixed programme, short visit, resort- based
3) Example of your own experience as a traveller and/or a tourist
4) Lessons learned
5) Applicability of lessons
6) Conclusion

What can be expected in a good response to quotation 4

4) *All travel has its advantages. If the traveller visits better countries, he may learn to improve his own; and if fortune carries him to worse, he may learn to enjoy his own.* Dr Johnson

1) Introduction: meaning of the quotation
2) Example one - travel to a 'better' country
    i)   Which country?
    ii)   What was 'better'?
    iii) How could you use this example to improve your own country?
3) Example two - travel to a 'worse' country
    i)   Which country?
    ii)   What was 'worse'?
    iii) What did you appreciate more about your own country?
4) What does it take to be able to use all travel experiences?

Conclusion: how can you use your experiences in future?

What can be expected in a good response to quotation 5

5) *See one promontory, one mountain, one sea, one river, and see all.* Socrates

As mentioned above, quotation 5 is open to several interpretations. It would be tricky to take the deepest interpretation as your starting point for this essay as you may have to think things through from the beginning and you have little time to do that. A simpler approach is to treat the meaning of the quotation in the same way as for quotation 3, that a true traveller needs to go beyond the sights of a place to learn about it. You could also tackle it from the perspective of quotations 1 and 2, that travel can induce lasting change in a person provided some engagement with the host society takes place.

Elizabeth *"Travel broadens the mind"*

①

'Travel broadens the mind.'
This assertion suggests that it is possible to expand upon one's awareness and experience through exposure to new places and societies encountered during travel. Given that our mental makeup is to a significant degree shaped by our environment, this seems like a reasonable assumption.

Having migrated to England at a young age, I can personally relate to this suggestion. Transition from a traditional Middle-Eastern society to a far more multi-dimensional Western European one exposed me to practices, ideologies and attitudes that could be construed as incorrect or blasphemous, for instance, in my country of birth. In particular, the diversity of religious faiths in Europe displaced an almost inborn notion that there was only one way to live. Consequently I was able to penetrate two very polar mindsets, and found that my tolerance levels generally grew to extremely high levels due to what became an insider's understanding on either side of the divide. Increased tolerance allowed for more objective observations of life, tainted less than would be expected with personal bias, and this has helped me hugely in interacting with and relating to people.

Despite this effect on myself, however, I have also witnessed instances where travel has had little to no impact on a person's mind. My father, for instance, who also travelled to England from the same social and cultural setting, as a young adult, seems to have remained largely resilient to the many aspects of the new environment. Despite decades of observation and integration, he remains true to opinions and beliefs that have stood the test of time and place. While his knowledge and practical experience may have broadened as a result of travel, his character and the fundamental personality component

②

of his mind are very difficult to influence with travel alone.

Based on anecdotal evidence such as this, I would conclude that while travel certainly does have the power to inform people and provide triggers for personal growth, it is not a formula for metamorphosis. Gain in knowledge or in spectrum of experience expands upon consciousness but breadth of mind also requires maturation of character, judgement or personality. Perhaps, in order for the mind to respond to travel in such a way, prerequisite abilities such as mental malleability and inherent flexibility with regards to others are required in order to overcome the hard-wired subjectivity and self-middedness that exists in some more than others. Endorsed with a more organic and open attitude to life, however, travel can indeed add new depth and angles to mentality. As such, it perhaps could be encouraged for the purpose of promoting awareness and inciting greater empathy between societies and peoples, especially at younger ages when the mind is still absorbing from the external social environment at a naturally high rate. If it has ever a small chance of facilitating the understanding worlds beyond the scope of one's own sphere of existence, travel can be very beneficial. and filling out one's observational skills.

Hello Erin! I started writing this as an expository essay, having mixed up which section was which & not reading section A properly, and this ended up as a mixture of both styles - also a bit long + general as a result.

85

This writer spotted her main error, namely that her writing in a large part of this essay is neither reflective nor personal but expository. The first part of her essay from the introduction to the top of the second page is reflective, while the second part is expository. She may not be penalised for this in the exam but I have marked it down because it does not fully meet the terms of the brief. In any event, she would need to make the point that moving to a new country can be considered an extreme form of travel.

Elizabeth gives enough of her own experiences and that of her father to show the reader that she has a grip on the intended content of the essay so if she had made this mistake in the exam, she may well have still scored reasonably well. Instead of more general comments, she could have explored why her experience differed so greatly from her father's and whether age, personality and receptivity to new ideas might also have played a part. Her conclusion is not based on the reflective part of the essay and she did not comment on her learning with respect to wider society. Elizabeth's use of language is very fluent and mature and she shows a mastery of expression.

Specific commentary
Thought and content (quality of thought and feelings)
Relevance to brief
Insightful
Elizabeth's introduction is conventional but nevertheless shows that she understands the meaning of the quotation. Given that she is not going to describe travel *per se* but an experience of moving from one country to another, this would have been a good place to mention her approach. The essay shows relevance to the brief albeit by choosing a move to another country as proxy for travel, demonstrating an extreme approach to the theme of travel. Her insight into the changes she underwent on moving country and the resistance of her father to the values of his adoptive country are intriguing and it would have been interesting to the reader had she explored these differences.

Thought and content (what is made of and developed from the task)
Assertions explained
Assertions backed up with evidence
Individual answer rather than expected answer
Coherent perspective

The assertions made in the first few paragraphs are explained, exemplified and elaborated so that the reader is absolutely clear of the writer's meaning. The examples Elizabeth chooses to show the reader two points of view are very good ones but she fails to explain the differences between the two people in the example. It is an individual rather than conventional response as it is so unusual and the perspective is coherent in that the thoughts flow logically. There is no mention of the wider relevance of her theme to society, which is a pity as the process of cultural adjustment of newcomers is pertinent to many societies.

Organisation and expression
Structure (shape and form)
Sufficient coverage of topic
Coherence within paragraphs
Paragraphs connected to each other
Paragraphs develop theme
Conclusion based on paragraphs

Elizabeth's essay has some coverage of a personal nature and it is enough to let the reader know she understands the brief. She does not appear to have made a plan as she veers off the personal aspects into a more discursive approach in the second half of the essay. Her coverage, therefore, is patchy. The paragraphs relating to the personal aspects are coherent and flow into one another with ease. The first three paragraphs are connected to each other and the fourth could have served as a conclusion as it is based on the preceding work but the essay continues past this logical end and begins a new theme.

Organisation and expression
Effectiveness and fluency of language
Good range of vocabulary
Appropriate use of language
Conventional grammar

As mentioned in the general commentary, this writer demonstrates fluent language skills: a wide vocabulary, excellent variety of sentence structure, and subtlety of expression. She misuses one word; in paragraph three, second sentence she describes her father as being 'resilient' to many aspects of the new environment. While this is an interesting word, 'resistant' might have been a better choice.

Marks out of 60
Thought and content

Relevance to brief	5/10
Insightful	7/10
Assertions explained	6/10
Assertions exemplified	6/10
Individual answer	6/10
Coherent perspective	5/10
TOTAL	**35/60**

Organisation and expression

coverage of topic	2/5
coherence of paragraphs	3/5
paragraphs connected	2/5
paragraphs develop theme	3/5
conclusion from paragraphs	2/5
good range of vocabulary	5/5
appropriate use of language	5/5
conventional grammar	5/5
TOTAL	**27/40**

Overall total	**62%**

Jean *"The advantages of experiences from travel"*

Jean p1

Writing Test B.

The advantages of experiences from travelling

Quote four "... travel has its advantages.... better countries ... learn to improve his own.... worse, he may learn to enjoy his own." is trying to explain that experiences gleaned from travelling can help people to reflect on aspects of their own life. I interpret this quote to mean that countries that are better, worse, at doing something than the country that I currently live in, England, that the country as a whole is better as this would be so personal and very vastly.

For example I recently visited Mauritius and found the integration of many different and opposing cultures far better than any other country I have had the pleasure to visit. This fascinated me as England is fairly good, but in my opinion, at accepting and attempting to integrate the cultures that we have but there are still many problems. I feel that perhaps due to the balance of the diversity of the people in Mauritius that this lends itself well to such an integration of the cultures. This has made me much more accepting and open to migration into England. agreement with the quote

Similarly, in when travelling in America I found it very difficult to find many healthy food options, especially "fast"

Jean p2

food. Whereas in England, I find it is much easier to find healthy and interesting food in many establishments. This is not really something I considered before travelling to America but now I really appreciate the choice available in England. I find it very difficult to think of any examples of my own life where some aspect of my travels has not been advantageous. This is not to say travel is not without its disadvantages, for example some travel is risky and I have been quite unwell, due to poor food hygiene, and had property stolen, in less secure environments. But, so many aspects of my travels has changed my views and opinions of my own country and I feel has enriched my life beyond how I may be without those experiences. Different people may glean completely different lessons from very similar experiences and as such travel experiences and personal growth greatly differ between people.

General commentary

By and large this is a competent essay in which the writer has addressed the question implicit in the quotation. Jean helpfully tells the reader to which quote she is referring and writes about some experiences of travel that made her appreciate her own country, giving two clear examples to illustrate her views. What is missing, however, is how she can relate her views about England to the wider society. Would she, for example, challenge those who complain about England? Would she try to learn why racial integration in Mauritius is so successful and tell others about it? That would be the better conclusion; Jean needs to remember that, for the exam the wider society must feature in both essay types. Her language is generally sound. The essay is rather scanty in its coverage and more detailed explanations would have served her better.

Specific commentary
Thought and content (quality of thought and feelings)
Relevance to brief
Insightful

Jean's essay is relevant to the brief in that she mentions two specific examples where she experienced aspects of life one of which was better and one of which was worse than in her own country. The example of cultural integration, assuming it is true, in Mauritius shows insight as she attempts to explain why this might be the case. She contrasts cultural integration in Mauritius with that of England and hazards a guess as to why this should be better in Mauritius. In other words, Jean has attempted to explain her experience fully. The example of food in the USA is not so satisfactory as she does not attempt to explain why the fast food in the USA and in England is so different and so does not demonstrate any insight into this phenomenon. Given the cultural mix in the USA, it is surprising that fast food is not good. This warrants some exploration of the causes but the writer does not do this.

Thought and content (what is made of and developed from the task)
Assertions explained
Assertions exemplified
Individual answer rather than expected answer
Coherent perspective

The introduction explains the meaning of the quotation and the writer elaborates upon this to show her own understanding of the meaning. She gives examples to show she has understood the meaning. The essay is rather pedestrian, particularly the example of fast food in the USA. There must be other examples she experienced which she could have used to better effect, such as the public transport system or the lack of a national health system as negative examples. Her perspective is coherent throughout as the last paragraph shows her general approach to lessons learned from travel.

Organisation and expression
Structure (shape and form)
Sufficient coverage of topic
Coherence within paragraphs
Paragraphs connected to each other
Paragraphs develop theme
Conclusion based on paragraphs

The coverage is rather scanty and incomplete given that her second example is not fully worked out. Her last paragraph is too general in nature to be considered fully part of the topic set out in the brief.

Each paragraph is self-contained and contains one thought which is explored to a lesser or greater degree. The paragraphs develop the theme of the brief and the conclusion attempts to draw on the preceding paragraphs but veers towards a more general conclusion, namely that all travel is advantageous, which misses the rest of the quotation.

Organisation and expression
Effectiveness and fluency of language
Good range of vocabulary
Appropriate use of language
Conventional grammar

Jean's use of language is simple, as is her vocabulary. There are a couple of lapses; her spelling of 'integrate' and use of the word, 'vastly' for 'a vast topic'. She makes no grammatical errors. Overall, the writing does not display the maturity one would hope for in an essay at this level so wider reading would help develop both vocabulary and language style.

Marks out of 60
Thought and content

Relevance to brief	7/10
Insightful	6/10
Assertions explained	6/10
Assertions exemplified	7/10
Individual answer	5/10
Coherent perspective	6/10
TOTAL	**37/60**

Organisation and expression

coverage of topic	4/5
coherence of paragraphs	4/5
paragraphs connected	4/5
paragraphs develop theme	4/5
conclusion from paragraphs	3/5
good range of vocabulary	2/5
appropriate use of language	2/5
conventional grammar	4/5
TOTAL	**27/40**

Overall total	**64%**

Lisa The traveller sees what he sees, the tourist sees what he has come to see. *GK Chesterton*

Lisa p1

B) "The traveller sees what he sees, the tourist sees what he has come to see"

To understand this statement it is important to have a grasp of the key words, traveller and tourist. A traveller is a person who has taken time off from their life to visit many other countries, over a prolonged period of time, frequently with no particular place in mind. "Blows in with the wind" is a phrase ~~that springs into my mind tourists~~ commonly associated with travellers. Conversely a tourist is a person that has taken annual holiday and chooses a particular destination, with the idea of seeing some famous landmarks of the country. The statement implies that a traveller will soak up the atmosphere and daily activities of the place, whereas the tourist will make a beeline from one tourist attraction to the next, oblivious of the life around him.

A personal example to illustrate this remark is on when I ~~trav~~ travelled by interrail around eastern europe for a month. I had no particular destination in mind, but arrived in Prague, once there I decided to remain ~~there~~ a week. As a traveller I had a lowly budget and could not afford to eat in expensive restaurants, as a planned tourist might. Instead I visited the local supermarket for food rations. It was in this mundane activity that I was struck by the differences in culture between

Lisa p2

here and my native England. It was the labelling
of the food and banter of the fellow customers
which made this city so different from my own. As a tourist
it would be possible to not experience such a
daily ~~experience~~ task as food shopping. ~~As you as~~
a result I was far more able to appreciate the
cultural differences between the two nations.

Nevertheless the following day I was waiting
at the bus stop when a Czech lady approached
me and asked which country I was from. Upon
my reply she began to jump up off the ground,
hands and hair flying, crying "Manchester
United, David Beckham" repeatedly. It was this
encounter which brought into sharp relief, that
despite the differences in nature between our two
countries, the human spirit has some universal
~~loved~~ pleasures!

From this example I can see that as a traveller
a person is much more likely to come away from
the experience with an appreciation of the lives
of ordinary citizens. Whereas a tourist may
arrive back home with a photo collection of the
elegant architecture, and an understanding of the
countries history. But all the things a tourist
has achieved the traveller will have too, and far
more.

In conclusion in order to become fully
immersed in a new situation it can be argued
that it is best to not have any preconceived
plans as to how to achieve this. Rather to
start the event and make your ~~conclusion~~ decision after
you have more comprehension of the ~~taste~~ place. This
will result in a far richer reward.

As a traveller I ~~becomes~~ become drenched in the local atmosphere
whereas a tourist always remains one step removed. As a
traveller - I was much more likely to become enriched, and
altered by ~~their~~ my experiences.

General commentary

Some of Lisa's introduction is apt but I am not sure that the number of countries visited marks out a traveller from tourist; it seems to be more to do with the attitude with which each type of visitor approaches a new place. I agree with Lisa that length of time may also be a factor in determining the extent to which a tourist can become a traveller; it may be hard to be a traveller if only a week or two is available. Nevertheless, the introduction makes a valid start. The essay fulfils this early promise with some relevant reflections on Lisa's own experiences as a traveller as opposed to a tourist. However, she omits the benefits her approach can have in future and the applicability of these to the wider society, for example, sharing her approach with friends or demonstrating in some other setting what she has learned from these experiences. Her writing is fluent and mature.

Specific commentary
Thought and content (quality of thought and feelings)
Relevance to brief
Insightful

Lisa shows that the key difference is in the respective meanings of the words 'tourist' and 'traveller'. She defines these two words showing relevance to the brief and demonstrates insight through her explanations and examples of the two types of visitor.

Thought and content (what is made of and developed from the task)
Assertions explained
Assertions exemplified
Individual answer rather than expected answer
Coherent perspective

Lisa explains her assertions thoroughly and gives detailed examples to show the differences in approach taken by the tourist and the visitor. Her first example, of being a visitor to Prague, is the most satisfactory since she shows how she 'travelled', that is, visited food markets. She does not explain how the food was labelled nor how this differed from food in English markets; she merely states the fact that food was labelled differently. She shows an understanding of the cultural differences that can be observed by a traveller. Lisa returns to the tourist experience by stating that her experience would not be accessible to tourists who concern themselves only with sightseeing.

Her second example, that of a football fan, is perhaps not so satisfactory as this experience may be similar to that of a tourist. Nevertheless, it is a useful example as she shows similarities in cultures through their interest in football. The perspective is coherent throughout as she balances the experiences of a tourist and a traveller.

Lisa's conclusion is rather long and has a piece tacked on which does not add much to the essay. However, she draws the essay together in her conclusion by showing that it is the attitude taken towards the host society that distinguishes the traveller from the tourist.

Organisation and expression
Structure (shape and form)
Sufficient coverage of topic
Coherence within paragraphs
Paragraphs connected to each other
Paragraphs develop theme
Conclusion based on paragraphs

There is certainly sufficient coverage of the topic. The essay is well balanced, the paragraphs are internally coherent and are connected to each other. Each paragraph takes the theme forward, leading to an insightful conclusion. There is no mention of the relationship between her experiences and wider society but she has learned lessons which will allow her to make the most of visits to other countries. The essay's conclusion is marred by the inserted paragraph; it is almost a second conclusion.

Organisation and expression
effectiveness and fluency of language
good range of vocabulary
appropriate use of language
conventional grammar

The language used is fluent and conveys the writer's intentions effectively. There are one or two lapses such as sentences that begin with 'whereas' or 'rather', which are usually used to join two sentences or phrases. There are also some unfortunate clichés: 'drenched in the local atmosphere', 'soak up the atmosphere' and 'beeline', for which 'absorbed' and 'head directly' could have been substituted. These are minor quibbles in what is an otherwise mature essay using varied language and a good range of vocabulary.

Marks out of 60
Thought and content

Relevance to brief	8/10
Insightful	8/10
Assertions explained	8/10
Assertions exemplified	7/10
Individual answer	8/10
Coherent perspective	8/10
TOTAL	**47/60**

Organisation and expression

coverage of topic	4/5
coherence of paragraphs	4/5
paragraphs connected	4/5
paragraphs develop theme	4/5
conclusion from paragraphs	3/5
good range of vocabulary	3/5
appropriate use of language	3/5
conventional grammar	2/5
TOTAL	**27/40**

Overall total	**74%**

Susan *Certainly, travel is more than the seeing of sights; it is a change that goes on, deep and permanent, in the ideas of living.*   *Miriam Beard*

Susan p.1

Writing Test B

1) "Certainly travel is more than just the seeing of sights, it is a change that goes on ..."

The statement is conveying that people learn things while travelling that can effect them for the rest of their lives. I have travelled to many places just to visit famous monuments or beautiful buildings, but often it is the people that I have met while travelling that I remember most fondly.

I travelled around North America and Canada for three months a few years ago with friends. We wanted to see all the sights, for example the spectacular falls in Niagra, and we suceeded in this and took some wonderful photos to remember them by. However, this would not have been possible if we did not have the kindness of strangers to rely upon.

On our first night staying at a remote campsite in Canada, it became extremely cold, and we did not have enough blankets and clothes to keep us warm. We had been talking to the owner of the camp earlier that evening and so we asked him if we could

us warm. We had been talking to the owner of the camp earlier that evening and so we asked him if we could borrow some clothes. He subsequently offered to take us into his house. This was wonderful, and was beyond any help we expected from a stranger. As we were cold and tired, ~~his~~ his help was greatly appreciated. ~~I will always remember~~

This was the most important memory of my trip. I make sure ~~that~~ whenever there are tourists in my country needing help, for example with directions, I always give it to them.

~~The friends ~~Most~~ that I made, and people that I met ~~remain~~ have remained in my memory for longer than any buildings or ~~sights~~ that I ~~saw~~ have.~~

★ This experience while travelling has taught me to be kinder to strangers in general. I felt vulnerable and sometimes lonely while travelling, and I know the value of a friendly face to talk to. The experience will stay with me for the rest of my life, and will always affect the way that I behave towards strangers. ~~It was an unexpected lesson to have learned something~~

General commentary

Susan makes an effective start by showing that she has captured the gist of the meaning of this quote. She should have been more explicit in describing the meaning of the word 'change' in respect of the places visited. It is not only the fond memories of people she takes away but some deeper change and she needs to refer to this in her introduction. She refers to the kindness of strangers during her visit to North America and how this lesson has changed the way she now responds to strangers. She has fulfilled minimally the terms of the brief but something is missing. An example of how she has helped a stranger would have enriched her essay. In general, her use of language is sound and her style fluent with only occasional clumsiness. The scrappy handwriting is annoying.

Specific commentary
Thought and content (quality of thought and feelings)
Relevance to brief
Insightful

Susan's opening statement is simple and effective and she demonstrates that she understands the meaning of the brief. She suggests that it is the people met on a journey that make learning and hence change possible but this is not elaborated upon fully so the reader is left wondering about the cause of the deep changes. Her insight is that it is people rather than places that make the difference.

Her second paragraph spends too long describing the country she visited which works against the theme, that of the people she met. This paragraph could have been omitted. She gives only one example of a deep change brought about by travel and, although she shows insight, one more example would have been helpful. Her essay is peppered with crossing out, which reveals that she is writing before thinking through her statements. This leads her to write two conclusions or one in which the idea is repeated. A second example would have prevented this repetition; there would have been no time in which to write the same thing twice.

Thought and content (what is made of and developed from the task)
Assertions explained
Assertions exemplified
Individual answer rather than expected answer
Coherent perspective

Susan explains her assertion in the first paragraph and gives a detailed example. It is a conventional answer, it is often noted that strangers have offered help. The perspective is coherent in that the example supports the theme but she has to stretch this example across the whole essay.

Organisation and expression
Structure (shape and form)
Sufficient coverage of topic
Coherence within paragraphs
Paragraphs connected to each other
Paragraphs develop theme
Conclusion based on paragraphs

There is, as already mentioned, insufficient coverage of the topic. This leads to an unbalanced feel whereas two examples would have given greater balance. The first paragraph leads to the next three paragraphs, including the conclusion, so there is coherence both within and between the paragraphs. The paragraphs develop the theme but more is needed to illustrate some deep change beyond mere assertions. As mentioned before, there are two concluding paragraphs, the second of which is the better.

Organisation and expression
Effectiveness and fluency of language
Good range of vocabulary
Appropriate use of language
Conventional grammar

The language used in this essay is simple throughout. This is not a problem but it can become wearing to the reader because of the lack of variation. The first sentence is clumsy: 'conveying that' does not read well; Susan should have used 'suggests' instead. She tends to sprinkle her essay with commas and this also hinders the smooth flow of the piece. There are few grammatical errors.

Marks out of 60

Thought and content

Relevance to brief	7/10
Insightful	7/10
Assertions explained	5/10
Assertions exemplified	4/10
Individual answer	5/10
Coherent perspective	6/10
TOTAL	**34/60**

Organisation and expression

coverage of topic	2/5
coherence of paragraphs	4/5
paragraphs connected	4/5
paragraphs develop theme	4/5
conclusion from paragraphs	3/5
good range of vocabulary	2/5
appropriate use of language	3/5
conventional grammar	4/5
TOTAL	**26/40**

Overall total	**60%**

Frequently Asked Questions

These questions are derived from those asked at Dr Prep workshops held between 2004 and 2006. See *www.drprep.net* for details.

How do I know which quotation to choose?

The quotations are always going to be around a common theme so to some extent it does not matter which you choose, you will be writing a response to all the quotations probably with a slant towards one or more of them.

I always get blocked before I write an essay. How do I start?

The simplest way to begin is to write down your chosen quotation and think about its meaning. Make a plan as outlined in Chapter 2. For your introduction, explain the meaning of the quotations and note any implications. Then follow your plan to produce the rest of the essay.

How do I get a balanced structure?

See chapter 2 to refresh your memory. Aim for a simple structure with an introduction, a couple of examples you can explain and elaborate upon, suitable counter-examples and a conclusion based on the preceding paragraphs and your structure will be sound. It is a good idea to draft the structure in the form of paragraph headings in advance of the writing so you do not veer away from the topic.

Do my examples have to be true?

No, you can make up examples if you can give them a ring of authenticity. It is easier to sound authentic if you have had the experience you are describing but it could have occurred to someone you know or be something you have seen or read about.

How do I link my paragraphs?

There are many useful linking words, for example: furthermore, however, nevertheless. You can also improve cohesion across paragraphs by repeating words or groups of words used in the previous paragraphs.

How do I know when to stop?

Keep an eye on the time. When you get to 7 or so minutes from the end of the exam, begin the conclusion which you planned during your preparation time. It is crucial that your conclusion does not appear to be tacked on, but is integral to the writing in the preceding paragraphs.

What about poor spelling?

As long as misspellings do not get in the way of your meaning, the penalty will be light. If you are not sure of a spelling, use a different word which you can spell with confidence.

Do you have to avoid the use of 'I' in an essay?

There is no harm in using 'I' sparingly in an expository essay. However, instead of saying something like, 'I think', just say what you think. For example, if you believe bear baiting is wrong, you do not have to say, 'I think bear baiting is wrong'. You can say ,'Bear baiting is wrong' and then justify your statement.

Use 'I' in the personal essay - it would be hard to imagine an essay of this type which doesn't do so.

How can I improve my style?

- Think before you write
- Keep punctuation simple
- Avoid dashes
- Vary the length of sentences
- Vary the beginning of sentences
- Signpost clearly any change of direction
- Stay active not passive
- Keep vocabulary simple

What are the most common errors?

Common mechanical errors are poor handwriting, crossing out or arrows indicating an omitted thought. Writing perpendicular to the lines in an attempt to include additional thoughts makes the work look untidy.

it include thin argument, undeveloped ideas, a xplained assertions and arguments without well as examples which are stated but not

expression include informal language, words ts for the reader, unconnected paragraphs, olly thinking), drifting off the topic, taking too ting a point made earlier.

ded with careful planning and thought before

se all of the official ACER sample paper ce essays in total.